ADVANCE PRAISE

— — —

"Managing corporate sales for Major League Baseball for over a decade, I struggle to create new ways to motivate and inspire my staff. Lisa's three-word approach is a simple yet effective tool that renews focus and helps reach goals."

—Bill Reinberger, Vice President, corporate sales,
Cincinnati Reds

"Sales meeting content is something every sales manager has struggled with. *Three Word Meetings* gives you great ideas on how to create a little fun, with a motivating tone everyone can rally behind. These are useful no matter what industry you are in."

—Bryson Lair, Sales Manager, Cincinnati Bell Business

"I've been in sales for over thirteen years, and in our industry, you have to think quickly, move quickly, and react quickly. I have often found that sales meetings slow me down. That is, until our first three-word meeting with Lisa. As a former sales person herself, she is able to keep our team focused without wearing us out with too much information. I find that *Three Word Meetings* stays with me throughout the week, inspires me to be a better sales person, and keeps me moving forward in my fast-paced world. Three words: Buy this book. It could change your meetings tomorrow!"

—*John Williams, WKRQ-2060 Digital*

"As a busy account executive, I've often felt there were better ways for me to spend an hour of my day than attending a sales meeting. Lisa's *Three Word Meetings* changed my opinion on this and, instead, provided me with a weekly meeting time to refocus and engage on a topic that delivered a meaningful and relevant message in a concise manner. No matter what the topic, I always find it insightful and relatable to my business."

—*Sara Minda Reardon, thirteen-year veteran Account Executive for WREW; WKRQ*

"Who wants to sit through another meeting? *Three Word Meetings* is a simple way to inspire and engage your audience! I walk out of every meeting thinking of better ways to improve my path. It offers a strategic way to think about my day and encourages me to reevaluate my systems and to improve my processes. I always leave meetings motivated and inspired."

—Jason Budzik, Senior Account Executive at
WKRQ-2060 Digital for eighteen years.

"There are so many ideas that can be summed up in three words: You did it! Go for it! One more try! I had never put much thought into the significance three words could have on my motivation for both work and my personal life, until I began working with Lisa. The way she elaborates the meaning behind three simple words always gets me to think differently, to open up my mind. Sales can be a frustrating job day to day, but solutions are just three words away in the eyes of Lisa. Are we prepared? Consistency pays off. Seize the moment. Lead the way. I owe a lot of my success to Lisa and the way she coaches me on finding a way to stay relevant with my clients and build those relationships, and she usually does it in three words or less. Thank you, Lisa.

—Emily Martin, WKRQ–2060 Digital
Senior Account Executive

THREE WORD MEETINGS

A Simple Strategy to Engage,
Inspire, and Empower Your Team

LISA THAL

RIVER GROVE
BOOKS

Published by River Grove Books
Austin, TX
www.rivergrovebooks.com

Distributed by River Grove Books

Design and composition by Greenleaf Book Group and Sheila Parr
Cover design by Greenleaf Book Group and Sheila Parr
Cover image: Shutterstock / ihor_seamless

Cataloging-in-Publication data is available.

Print ISBN: 978-1-63299-096-9

eBook ISBN: 978-1-63299-097-6

First Edition

This book is dedicated to all the managers, leaders, and clients who took the time to care about my career and to invest their time and talent in me. I am grateful. Thank you for making a difference in my career and my life.

Instructions for success:
1) Read this book.
2) Implement the ideas.
3) Buy more copies.

CONTENTS

PREFACE

— — —

The future of your organization and the performance of your team can hinge on one weekly sales meeting. It's a simple theory: The people we engage, inspire, and empower each week can determine our success. This realization came to me while participating in a meeting where I witnessed various attempts to capture the attention of those in the room. So how can we create weekly meetings that give the salesperson value, purpose, and fun?

What I have come to know over my thirty-year career is that leaders want to engage and empower others. They want to be able to navigate the various personalities in the room and lead them with one common goal in mind—to inspire them! The content and words we choose so carefully are critical to capturing our teams' attention and encouraging them to do more than they ever thought possible for themselves. I wrote *Three Word Meetings* to help you become more productive and consistently create excitement around your weekly meetings.

Each chapter focuses on three words to use as a discussion prompt during your sales meetings. In each chapter, I discuss the concept of the three-word phrase and how you might implement it. Next, I share a case study about how those three words were used in the field. Then, there is section titled "For You," which walks you through how the three words apply to you, the team leader. Finally, there is a section "For Your Team," which provides a series of questions to encourage your team to engage with how the three words apply to them and their clients.

During my career in media, I understood the power of marketing. I was most impressed by concise taglines that conveyed action: Nike's "Just Do it"; McDonald's "I'm lovin' it"; and GEICO's "15 minutes could save you 15% or more on your car insurance." These marketing phrases had me lacing up my running shoes and heading to McDonald's in my car, while saving 15 percent on my car insurance with GEICO.

I realized that if I could find a way to engage my team each week with a simple and focused message, then perhaps they would be inspired personally and professionally to do the same with their clients. Each week I evaluated where my team was and then determined the three words I might use during our meeting. If they needed inspiration that week, I would use "Live Your Dream!" If they needed focus, then I would use "Win the Day!" I would build my entire sales meeting around those words. I would share the three words, go over our business needs, and then circle back to the three words and what I wanted to achieve that week. The meetings had purpose, they became fun, and the sales team started looking forward to them.

It has become my mission to help other leaders create better weekly meetings. I understand the daily demands on managers, and I hope this book will help you save valuable time and inspire you along the way. It is my hope that you find the book to be a simple yet major resource for you.

INTRODUCTION

— — —

Let's face it: Meetings suck! They suck figuratively, as in: "These meetings are sucking the life out of me!" And, they suck literally, as in:

- More than a third of work time is spent in meetings.
- Managers attend more than sixty meetings per month.
- Nearly 50 percent of all business people think meetings are a waste of time.
- 39 percent of participants admit to dozing off during meetings.
- 70 percent of participants admit to bringing other work to meetings.
- The cost of wasted meeting time is estimated at nearly $40 billion.[1]

---

1 Edwin Siebasma, "$37 billion per year in unnecessary meetings, what is your share?," *Meetingking.com,* October 21, 2013.

Conservatively, I estimate that I have attended more than three thousand meetings in my thirty-year sales career. In the early years, I attended as a seller, sitting somewhere near the back of the room. Perhaps, on occasion, I'd drift. Many times I brought other work. Thankfully, Facebook did not exist back then; otherwise I could have been out of a job a long time ago.

I have participated in many more meetings as a sales manager. On a certain level, it is more stressful to be standing at the front of the room. Any good leader wants to run a meeting that brings a sense of purpose to the team. Good leaders want to connect with their work family, to make a difference. But it is difficult. If you run a weekly sales meeting, it is challenging to have something interesting or engaging to talk about every week. It is difficult to keep the team energized.

The obvious answer to this dilemma may seem to be that if they are so difficult maybe you should cut down on the number of meetings you have. This may be a simple answer, but it's not the correct answer. I believe that weekly sales meetings serve an important purpose. The people around you are called a sales *team*. I've always taken the word "team" seriously during my years as a sales manager. A team needs to be cohesive, needs to feed off of each other. As a sales manager, I felt it was important to bring my team together at least once a week to create a sense of community. They came together to share experiences and the challenges they faced. It wasn't always easy to create a sense of community, because many people naturally have short attention spans, especially these days with smart phones and iPads to provide distraction. Even with my best intentions, I was challenged to run a meeting that left my team feeling inspired, motivated, or engaged.

All of that changed one Sunday afternoon three years

ago when a Nike commercial came on during the sporting event I was watching on TV. As with all Nike commercials, the final image is their iconic swoosh and their even more iconic tagline: "Just Do It." It is possible that it is one of the greatest advertising slogans of all time. Not only did it help create one of the world's great brands, but it also inspired an entire generation of aspiring weekend warriors to tie up their Nikes and hit the pavement or the basketball court or the tennis court. "Just Do It" became a clarion call for people of all ages to get up off the sofa and start taking care of themselves.

That commercial gave me an idea. Perhaps I could take what Nike did with three words and use it to somehow motivate or energize my sales team. Most importantly, perhaps I could use three words to give our weekly sales meeting a sense of purpose.

When my team assembled for the Monday morning sales meeting I walked in and wrote three words on the white board: "It's All Possible." I told them to let the phrase stew in the back of their minds because we were going to talk about the meaning of the words after getting through some of our basic administrative subjects. I purposely got through the basics quickly because I was curious to see if my three-word experiment would have any impact on the team. What happened next exceeded my expectations.

Everyone jumped into the conversation, contributing their own perspective and ideas as to what "It's All Possible" meant to them. We then directed the conversation to how the phrase translated to their work as sellers. How could "It's All Possible" improve their outreach efforts? How could the phrase help them deal with clients whom they'd always deemed impossible? The energy in the room was palpable.

We somehow turned a mundane sales meeting into an impromptu training exercise using three interlocking words. It was our "Just Do It" moment.

The three-word exercise is now a standard element in my meetings. I've found that sellers look at the board as soon as they enter the room to see what the week's phrase will be. The meetings have been transformed into an energetic exchange of ideas, creating the kind of cohesion and community that I always hoped for in sales meetings but rarely realized.

Based on the success I've had with the three-word exercise, I wanted to share my experience. I've included fifty-two three-word phrases for your weekly meetings. Each chapter includes the phrase along with some background on its relevance to our culture as well as my thoughts on how the phrase can be incorporated into a discussion about selling. I have also included prompts to extend the conversation in each meeting.

I've found two effective ways to use the three-word exercise: You can simply have the three words available at the beginning of each meeting and then get to the discussion after covering your essential agenda topics. Or you can send your team the three words in advance of the sales meeting to give them some time to think about what the phrase means to them. Either way, I'm certain you will find the exercise a welcome addition to your sales meeting culture.

The topics are not listed in any particular order. Feel free to move around in the book and discuss topics you feel would most benefit your team in any given week.

I wish you luck with your meetings and hope you have as much success with the three words as I have had. As I say at the beginning of each of my sales meetings: Let's get started!

Chapter 1

LEAD THE WAY

— — —

We use "lead the way" in many different contexts. Let's take a look at two of the most common interpretations:

1. Act as a guide in advance of others; go first to show someone the way: "He led the way on point as we made our way through the jungle."

2. Be first or most prominent in some field or action: "She led the way for the US Olympic team with three gold medals."

One of our great debates revolves around the question of whether leaders are born or made. It is obviously easy to track the success of leaders over time and ascribe such success to their schooling or training. But does genetics come into play? This was the great mystery until several years ago when a study was published by University College London.[2] It was

---

2 Tim Elmore, "Are Leaders Born or Made?," *growingleaders.com*, January 25, 2013.

the first time researchers could show a link between certain genetic traits and leadership. The study did not dispute the fact that leadership skills can be learned, but it was the first time a scientific study showed that leadership qualities could be passed down through generations.

When we ask someone to lead the way, we are making a number of statements about their character:

- We are saying we trust them based on their previous performance.

- We are saying we believe that they have our best interests in mind.

- We are saying that we know they've gone down this path before, and we are comfortable with their guidance.

- We are saying that we think we can learn from their experience.

- We are saying that we appreciate the fact that they have been successful in the past and we want to gain from those successes.

When I was managing a radio station, we were faced with a dip in our ratings and the onset of a recession. The combination was going to take us down a path I didn't want us to go down. My sales team was compensated with a 100 percent commission plan. In the radio industry one rating point dip could mean thousands in lost revenue from the advertising agencies and lost commissions for my team. I knew we would have to work through the dip in ratings, and so I needed to figure out a solution to how my sales team could earn other commissions to offset the agency side of their business. I decided to lead the way on generating direct business, which was not impacted by ratings. The easiest way to do this was to show them how to do it, instead of telling them how to do it. I hit the streets on my own, as I had created a list of direct clients and met with them individually over the coming weeks.

When I started to quickly make sales, their curiosity led them to ask me what I was doing, so I happily played them the sample commercials (spec spots) and customized proposals I put together for these businesses, which I had titled: "Recession-Buster Programs to Grow Your Market Share." If their market was going to have fewer opportunities due to the recession, I needed to find a solution for my clients to capture a larger share of the available market. I would have faced the typical pushback if I had shoved the concept on my team; but by doing it myself first and leading the way it was an easy conversion from customized programs. The sales team sold more, earned higher commissions, and the company's annual revenue increased.

For You

- Think about someone who you believe to be a great leader and discuss the qualities you admire in that person.
- What are the ways you can serve as an example and lead the way in your current role?
- Do you feel confident when leading your team?
- How do you inspire others to lead the way?

For Your Team

Ask your team to share their thoughts on what the phrase "Lead the Way" means to them.

Next, expand the discussion using the following prompts:

- Think about someone who you believe to be a great leader and discuss the qualities you admire in that person.
- What leadership traits do you believe you have?
- In what circumstance has someone asked you to lead the way?
- How does the phrase "Lead the Way" play out in your client relationships?
- What are the ways you can serve as an example and lead the way in your current role?

"A leader is one who knows the way, goes the way, and shows the way."

—*John Maxwell*

Chapter 2

IN THE ZONE

— — —

A popular phrase in the American vernacular, especially in reference to professional sports, is "in the zone." NBA stars who are on a hot streak from beyond the three-point line claim to have been in the zone. Baseball players in the midst of a hitting streak tell how the ball seems bigger and slower, almost impossible not to hit, when they are in the zone.

Michael Jordan was once interviewed about what happens during particularly pressure-packed moments of important games. He said that whether at home or away, while in the zone he was almost in a place of total quiet. He became so totally focused on being in that moment of the game that everything else seemed to fall to the background or was shut out, including the noise of the crowd.

Being in the zone is actually a psychological concept known as flow. According to Wikipedia, flow is "a mental state of operation in which a person performing an activity is fully immersed in a feeling of energized focus, full involvement, and enjoyment in the process of the activity. In essence, flow is characterized by complete absorption in what one does."[3]

Being in the zone means there are three conditions at play:

1. We are solely focused on our goal and the actions needed to accomplish the goal, and it feels effortless.

2. We need immediate feedback so we can make adjustments to maintain the process and flow.

3. We must maintain our confidence through the process. We are energized by the entire experience.

Those who are frequently in the zone talk about feeling a sense of calm when all else around them may be chaos.

In the zone, or flow, is an excellent topic to explore with your team during a sales meeting. Every seller, especially those at the top of their game, has had moments when everything is going right, when every call clicks, when they might feel superhuman. They probably don't know it, but they are experiencing flow, or the sense of being in the zone.

For You

- Come up with a "zone moment" you may have had, either on the job or in your personal life. How did it feel?

- Think about a typical day. What aspects of your job are most likely to be those that create zone moments?

---

3   "Psychology," *wikipedia.org*, Accessed May 19, 2016.

- How can you create more zone moments during a typical day?

- What is happening in your body when you are in a zone moment?

- How do you think fear plays into zone moments?

For Your Team

Ask your team to share their thoughts on what the phrase "In the Zone" means to them.

Next, use the prompts you used in your exercise with your team.

*Change your perspective and you can
change your life.*

Chapter 3

LIVE YOUR DREAM

— — —

Let's be clear: There is a big difference between "living your dream" and the much-used phrase "living the dream." We've probably all used the phrase "living the dream" at some point, especially in those moments when life or work—or both—are conspiring to frustrate and bring us down. But for the purpose of this book, we will focus on the more positive one: "living *your* dream." We live in a country that embraces the belief that any person can accomplish any dream or goal through a commitment to hard work and perseverance.

The truth is we are born into a world that embraces this ethos, despite its imperfections. Little children are taught to think about what they want to be when they grow up. We need to make certain that we stay focused on living our dream—the life we have planned for ourselves with the goals in mind that we hope to achieve.

Of course, there are limits to living your dream. One can practice golf twenty-four hours a day for years and not approximate the success of Tiger Woods. And very few of us have the looks or talent to become an Oscar-winning performer. To that end, living your dream is framed by more achievable goals: a steady job, a family, a nice home, etc.

One day I noticed that one of my salespeople seemed distracted. I asked him if he was okay. He shared that his father had been ill and that the two had always had a strained relationship. His father was a successful surgeon, and the salesman's brother had followed in his footsteps. His father had taught his sons that living the dream was all about financial success, big homes, and vacations. This was not the dream my coworker saw for himself; but despite those feelings, he chose a career in sales, which was met with disapproval. He felt in sales he could still earn a great income without losing his authentic self. I asked him if he was happy selling. He shared that he loved the people he worked with, but he had always dreamed of being in a band and owning his own consulting company. He was never comfortable in a corporate setting with rules and expectations. He was more of a free spirit, and he felt that characteristic had faded over the past twelve years. He didn't want to disappoint his father, especially now that he was ill.

I expressed my sorrow that his father wasn't doing well, and I explained that perhaps the moment was for him. He needed to live his dreams and stop fulfilling someone else's. Life has a way of shifting us to where we need to go next. I asked him to take as much time as needed to determine if working in sales was where he should be. Weeks later he turned in his resignation. You could see that an emotional weight had been lifted off of him as he found the courage to start living his dream.

For You and Your Team

This is an interesting topic to explore with a sales team. It's likely that few, if any, sellers could say they are living their dream, that they grew up wanting to be a great salesperson. You do risk the chance that this discussion could prompt one or more of your sellers to realize they are missing their dream, in which case they might resign to become a bartender in Barbados.

Explore what "Live Your Dream" means with your team by using these prompts:

- How do you define "Live Your Dream"?
- On a scale of 1–10, with 10 being "fully living my dream," how would you rate your life and why?
- How important is money to living your dream?
- What can you do to help your clients live their dreams?

Don't dream your life, live your dream!
If don't live your dream, then you're
fulfilling someone else's.

Chapter 4

THE V FORMATION

Teamwork is a vital part of a thriving work environment. Everyone plays a critical role in the overall success of a company. Teamwork helps employees build trusting relationships with their coworkers, reduces workplace fatigue, and increases overall productivity. In sales your days can be filled with very high moments of interactions with clients and closing sales, along with the frustrations of not being able to connect to the decision maker on a potential account or losing a big sale. How do great sales teams consistently perform better than their competitors? They realize the importance of everyone's contributions to the overall team's success. They understand at any given time they may be asked to lead the team and accept that leadership role. The efforts of teams often produce far greater results than individuals.

How can you coach your team to work better together in order to produce better results? A great example of teamwork is how geese fly in the V formation and the valuable lessons the formation teaches us about working together.

1. **Teamwork:** By flying together in a V formation, the flock, scientists estimate, can fly about 70 percent farther with the same energy than if they flew alone. This is because each goose provides additional lift and reduces air resistance for the goose flying behind them. When everyone works together they too can arrive at their destination quicker and easier because everyone is contributing. Each team member is doing his or her part for the team. Is it possible to improve your teamwork?

2. **Effort:** When a goose decides to drop out of the line, it discovers that it requires more effort to fly. This happens because the goose loses its advantage of the lifting power that comes from flying together. You may experience members of your team falling behind and going on their own. They quickly find out that it is more fun to be on a team. It's more rewarding when their efforts contribute to the greater good of the team. Is everyone on your team giving their best effort?

3. **Leadership:** Each goose will be asked to take their turn in the front of the formation and lead the others. Each goose, like our team members, has an opportunity to step up and lead. Everyone has the opportunity to be a leader on the team given the chance. Can more leaders be developed?

4. **Communication:** The geese honk while they are flying to encourage each other along the way. They keep their lines of communication open so everyone knows the outcome. How is the communication with your team?

One year my team and I shared a vision of breaking an annual revenue goal for our company. We knew exceeding this goal was going to take tenacity and teamwork. We established the goal and strategized the game plan and effort it would require from each of us. Everyone understood that in order to achieve the goal they would each have to achieve their individual goal or, better yet, exceed their goal in case another seller fell short. We created a big board with our vision on it and hung it in the sales area as a reminder of what we were striving for. The revenue goal would get updated at the end of each week so the team knew how much more they had to produce. Each team member's name was listed—from the twenty-year veteran to the newest member who joined the team just sixty days before. It was exciting to watch how the veteran would encourage the newest member to contribute and step in to help if they faced setbacks. The team understood that at various times throughout the year each of them would need to step to the front and lead. They would high-five each other and ring a bell when a sale was added to the board. The energy and communication were contagious. We understood that we could encounter setbacks, but we were willing to keep pushing forward. We met our goal in the eleventh month of the year and celebrated our accomplishments. We shared what we learned through the process and realized that because of everyone's efforts, our goal was fulfilled.

For You

- Write down an example of when your team exceeded expectations.
- Write down an example of a time your team fell short.

- How can you improve the overall performance of your team?
- What strategies can you implement to improve your team's efforts?
- How do recognize and reward great teamwork?
- Do you have someone on your team who keeps your team from moving forward?

For Your Team

Ask your team to share their thoughts on what the phrase "The V Formation" means to them.

Next, walk them through the following:

- Write down positive and negative views you have about teamwork.
- What role do you play on the team?
- Share an example of how you contributed to the success of the team.
- Think of an example of when you took the responsibility to lead the team.
- How do you encourage other team members?

"Outstanding people have one thing in common: an absolute sense of mission."

—*Zig Ziglar*

Chapter 5

THE GROWTH
MINDSET

Our mindset is the single most important part of the sales process. If you're in sales, you can encounter various situations that you mentally have to be prepared for at all times. Your current mindset may be focused on preparation for the call, determination to close the account, or overcoming the objections to win the business. Through all our sales experiences, we have the ability to learn something new.

The good news is that you are the only one who can determine your mindset every moment and every day. When we set our minds to something, we feel more in control. When we set our minds on something we really want, we find a way to deliver on it.

Our minds are powerful; they can change the way we feel, the way we interpret a situation, the way we think, and what we are willing to do in any given moment. We also have the ability to shift our focus and go in another direction mentally if necessary. I am always looking for ways to grow personally and professionally. I was looking for a way to become a better communicator and public speaker. I walked through the following process to understand what I was trying to achieve. I asked myself:

1. **What outcome am I looking for?** I wanted to learn how to be a better communicator with my team and clients. I also wanted to learn how to be a more confident public speaker and presenter in business.

2. **Why do I want to do this?** The emotional reason why is that on occasion I would get a little nervous before speaking in public. I understood that most people feel that way when asked to speak in public. Like most things in life, if you practice and put yourself in an uncomfortable position, you will learn from each experience.

3. **What action do I need to do?** I did some research and discovered an eight-week Dale Carnegie course. The course was taught after work from 6:00–9:00 p.m. once a week. I made the commitment, and the learning began. I connected with other business professionals in the class who had the same vision. During the eight-week period we discussed various topics, from building a foundation for success to inspiring others in business. It created an environment for us to speak each week in front of a group about different topics. At the end of the course, I could sense how far each of us had progressed over the training. One of the biggest growth experiences was that it took a mindset of determination. We couldn't just show up each week without putting in the work. We had assignments, and we had to apply what we learned and build upon it in the workplace.

Many people have the same desire, but merely have intention and not commitment. Because I was determined, I gained an enormous benefit for myself. Every time I am asked to speak in public or be a part of a presentation in front of a large group, I am reminded of that eight-week experience that built self-confidence and a winning mindset.

For You

- Do you approach each day with a growth mindset?
- What action steps might you take to further develop your outcomes?
- Have you identified a plan of growth personally and professionally for yourself?
- What mind shifts can you make to further your growth?

For Your Team

Ask your team to share their thoughts on what the phrase "The Growth Mindset" means to them.

Next, ask them to share their experiences of when they set their mind to something. Did their mind create a solution for what they were focused on achieving? Did they close a big account? Earn their dream job? Obtain their promotion? Purchase their dream car? New home? Go on a much-dreamed-about vacation? Complete a marathon?

Ask your team the following three questions that will help shape their mindset toward growth and get them (and you!) the outcomes you desire:

1. **What's your outcome? What do you really want?** Is it growing your sales? How much income growth do you need to generate from those sales? Do you want to expand your skill sets to be top in your industry? Do you want to improve your work-life balance? Do you want to develop as a manager? Do you desire to stretch yourself so you can grow by getting out of your comfort zone?

2. **What is your purpose? Why do want it?** *Why* is another important question to ask yourself. It's the emotional reason behind why you do what you do. It's your mind that sets the agenda of why it is critical for you to accomplish your outcome, why it's a must for you. What will you gain or lose if you don't achieve your outcomes? What kind of stress would be eliminated when you get to your outcomes?

3. **What actions must you take to make this happen?** It's time to get to work! Design a strategy for growth and determine what you need to do each day that can lead to your outcomes. A driven mindset with timelines is imperative for you to continue your path of growth. Is it possible to tap into other employees with talent and skill sets to assist you getting there?

"What you believe affects what you achieve."
—*Bill Gates*

Chapter 6

ON THE RISE

— — —

"On the Rise" might be the richest and most compelling three-word meeting prompt in this book. That's because it implies that we are rising from a low point toward a new beginning. Perhaps it is from a personal tragedy. Or from a business failure. Or from a broken relationship. Think about sellers who are rejected nine out of ten times. That is a lot of low points!

Let's take a look at "On the Rise" from the perspective of failure. We put a lot of negative weight on failure in our culture, because failure is the yin to success's yang. But here's what's interesting: Contrary to belief, successful people will tell you that their success is not tied to repeatedly failing. They frame their success as repeatedly trying something, even if that attempt does not succeed.

Think about Thomas Edison. He attempted to create the light bulb more than a thousand times. Most people would quit at ten—or fewer. But Edison believed that our minds are capable of anything, so failure was only the impetus to try new approaches.

This leads us back to sellers. The best sellers love the pitch, regardless of how many times they are rejected. They are driven by being in the game. They inherently understand that they must possess the ability to rise up from their repeated defeats and that those defeats—those rejections—are not personal.

When my position managing a group of radio stations was eliminated, I thought my twenty-year career in broadcasting may have come to end. I loved the industry and was driven by coaching others. The financial reward was driven by my ego and the identity affiliated with the media industry I had created along the way. I remember driving home that day in the rain wondering what would be in store for me. My mindset could have been defeat, disappointment, or anger, but I had a feeling of calmness and trust that everything was in its divine order, even though I had no idea what was in store for me. I had a non-compete clause that allowed me ninety days to discover whether I would remain in media or explore another career path. One thing I was clear on was that I loved coaching people—whether it was sellers, on-air talent, clients, or others. It was clear I passionate about this, and my position had allowed me to coach others every day.

I decided to enroll to be certified as a life coach. I received a call from a company that I'd worked for eighteen years before, and they had a management opportunity available at a radio station for coaching a sales team of six. I accepted the opportunity and finished my certification to become a life coach. I wrote a book, *Why I Chose You*, during that year, as I was passionate in helping others discover why they chose those in their lives and the lessons we learn from experiences—whether those experiences are good or bad. I often reflect on how grateful I am for what appeared to be a setback but turned out to be an amazing gift. I was able to rise again with more clarity and confidence.

For You

- Think about a time when you have been defeated in life or in your job. What did you have to do and how long did it take before you were on the rise?
- Is there someone you admire who you witnessed reaching a low point only to rise up beyond your expectation?
- What did you learn from that experience?
- How do you feel when you find a way to rise up when faced with adversity?

For Your Team

Discuss what "On the Rise" means to your team by using these prompts:

- Think about a time when you have been defeated in life or in your job. What did you have to do and how long did it take before you were on the rise?
- How do you feel about being rejected, and what steps do you take to let it bounce off of you?
- Think about someone you know who was down and out. How did they rise up from their low point, and what can you learn from their experience?

What defines us is how well we rise after falling.

Chapter 7

ENGAGE, INSPIRE, EMPOWER!

Think back to the time when you accepted your first management position. If you were like me, you were extremely excited about the opportunity, even though you lacked the hands-on management experience. You were successful selling, and you now had the opportunity to coach others. The one thing you were confident about was that you wanted the ability to engage, inspire, and empower others. You were investing in the one commodity that would produce a major return on your time and talent—human capital.

In most companies we hire sales talent and have them download all the product knowledge we can fill their brains with in a very short period. Then we encourage them to use that knowledge and start converting sales from that experience. We are there to engage our team by listening to them in our weekly one-on-one meetings, creating conversations when in the field, making calls together, and asking thought-provoking questions to make them better. In doing so we share our best practices so they can hone their skills at a faster pace.

We are there to inspire them as well. We invested in them, and we want them to know through our interactions that they have our support.

Finally, our ultimate outcome is to empower them. We have invested the time by teaching them the skills and giving them the tools to lead themselves. We have given them everything they need to do the job successfully. Our expectation is that they in return engage, inspire, and empower others.

I just hired Charley to join our team. She had a few years of sales experience in another industry but not in media sales. It was my outcome to make certain she was prepared to be successful in the position. Don't get me wrong; she had a responsibility to use her skills and talent to generate revenue for our company as well. However, I recalled how the first day at my first sales position my manager gave me the business Yellow Pages and said, "Here is your new account list." I told myself that if I ever had the chance to become a manager, I would coach my team differently.

I had her set up a new business meeting and made the call. Doing so allowed her to see how I prepared for the call and to hear the thought-provoking questions I asked and the way I earned the second meeting by presenting a solution to the problem I'd uncovered. Once she was making calls on her own, we walked through each, and I asked what she learned from the call and what she would do differently to improve the call if she could make it again. We followed this process through several new meetings.

Next we made a call together. We discussed upfront who would lead what portion of the call and how we would feed off each other. We would follow this process through several calls as well. Finally, she led the entire call, and I stayed close by for support.

What was exciting for me was seeing the tremendous amount of confidence and improved skills gained from my taking the time to teach in the field. It engaged my seller, who was inspired by each call and was soon empowered to make them on her own with great confidence.

For You

- How do you engage with your team?
- Are there opportunities to create more time to engage with your team?
- How do you inspire your team?
- Are you enthusiastic and passionate about your role?
- Are there moments you can create to coach/teach your team?
- Do you have a clear direction and path to obtain that goal and do you have the tools to achieve it?

For Your Team

Ask your team to share their thoughts on what the phrase "Engage, Inspire, Empower!" means to them.

Next, ask them the following questions:

- How do you engage with your clients?

- Are there opportunities to create more time to engage with your clients or new prospects?
- How do you inspire yourself?
- Are you enthusiastic and passionate about your role?
- Have they created a clear direction and path to obtain the goal and have you given them the tools to achieve it?

"Leaders don't create followers, they create more leaders."

—*Tom Peters*

Chapter 8

SOMEDAY IS TODAY

— — —

Have you ever said any of the following?

- "Someday, I'll get my finances in order and get out of debt."
- "Someday, I will save enough money to retire."
- "Someday, I will start writing the great American novel."
- "Someday, I'll find a job I love."
- "Someday, I'll meet the woman/man of my dreams."

We love using the word "someday." But the problem with someday is that it is *not* today! We only have today to live whatever dream we may be holding. We only have today to do the most important work, the work that counts, the work that can't be put off.

Tomorrow is about procrastination, about avoiding what needs to be done today for any number of reasons. What sales manager has not heard these lines from their most ardent procrastinators? "I'll make ten more cold calls tomorrow." "I work much better when I'm on a tight deadline." "I'm not worried; I have a week to make my numbers."

I was successfully managing a group of radio stations in Cincinnati. It was an amazing experience, as I had the ability to work with some of my very best friends every day. I was director of sales, one step from the top management position, which was general manager. These positions rarely became available, and moving to another market was not something I was willing to do.

While on a client-incentive trip with our best customers, I received a phone call from my prior boss. He wanted to talk to me about a management position he had in mind for me with another radio company. I told him I was extremely happy with my current company and that I really appreciated him thinking of me. He asked me to hear him out and if, after meeting with him, I felt it was not a position I was interested in then he would understand.

He did pique my interest, so I met with him. He was being promoted to a regional VP and wanted me to take his general manager position. I was excited until reality set in. I couldn't leave my friends and coworkers whom I had been working with for so many years. He knew me well and asked that I take a few days to let the opportunity sink in. I spent the next two days thinking about the opportunity I had dreamed about. Accepting it would mean working with a new group of people and losing the ability to work with some of my best friends. After much reflection, I decided that the "someday" was today, and I accepted the position. It was a dream position, and I realized I had been preparing myself for this opportunity over the past twenty years.

For You and Your Team

This three-word exercise is an excellent way to get your team thinking about how they might minimize procrastination and learn how to live more in the moment. Start with procrastination. Ask your team if they identify with any of these procrastinator types:

- **Thrill-seekers.** They wait until the last minute to get things done, creating stress for themselves and anybody around them.

- **Avoiders.** They adopt the "out of sight, out of mind" attitude, hoping against hope that the task or project will magically go away.

- **Non-deciders.** They subscribe to the "analysis paralysis" theory of life and become obsessed with minimizing risk before moving forward.

"Someday Is Today" requires us to focus on this moment, to avoid procrastinating. In today's digitally obsessed world, it has become more difficult than ever to stay focused on the present moment. We are overwhelmed with stimulation and distractions. When discussing this topic with your team, suggest some very simple exercises to help them stay focused on today:

- Focus on their breath; practice deep-breathing exercises.

- When talking to someone (especially a client), be present; focus on that person's eyes.

- Put down your smart phones and tablets; stop checking Facebook. Simply unplug.

- What is your "someday" fantasy or dream?
- What are some ways you can change some of these procrastination habits?
- What are some ways you can practice being more present and make it a habit in your life?

To be great someday you have to start today!

Chapter 9

WHAT TO IMPROVE

— — —

Golf is a game of inches. It has numerous variables that influence play, including the temperature, precipitation, putting surface, and the type of grass you play on. Most sports, including football, baseball, swimming, bowling, biking, and running are won by inches. Taking the time to improve your performance by a small amount can give you a large reward.

What would it mean to you and your income if you made inches of improvement? We all can agree that to improve takes time, commitment, and practice. The best leaders in their industry don't just show up. They show up early, and they are well prepared to face any situation. They have practiced various outcomes so that they can remain at the top of their field. They draw upon their experiences to gain confidence.

An account executive that worked on my team had challenges staying organized. His desk was a disaster—with files literally taking over his workspace. I met with him to ask how I could help create a better organizational system.

He shared that he had great intentions of keeping his space organized but always became absorbed in working on various projects. It was an area he wanted to improve on, and he was willing to look for solutions. We discussed how more productive and efficient he would be if he could locate folders or details regarding his clients faster. He understood that getting organized was a process and that it would take his attention. He made the decision that he would come in on the weekend to go through the folders on his desk and create an organizational system that would work best for him.

When I saw his desk the following Monday, I wondered if we had hired a new salesperson. He felt like a weight had been lifted off him, and he was certain he would be more productive knowing where everything was located. He made a decision to keep his workspace organized by tidying it up at the end of each day. He also took an Outlook class online to organize his business more effectively so he could eliminate the files piling up on his desk altogether.

For You and Your Team

There's always room for improving your performance. Read and share with your team the following solutions for improving performance:

- When was the last time you invested your money—not the company's money—on becoming a better employee? Most salespeople have never purchased a sales book. Why? Doctors, lawyers, and accountants continuously educate themselves. Why shouldn't a salesperson? Invest in yourself!

- Google has changed the landscape. You can now learn at least a little bit about any topic you can think of, from prospecting and industry trends to competing companies and more about the person you will be meeting with. Better yet, invest in sales or motivational podcasts and MP3s that you can listen to on your way to work and at home.
- Ask the top people in your field what they do to be leaders in their industry.
- Take classes online.

Next, with your team, list the areas of their games where they feel they could improve. Ask them:

- Could you be more organized?
- Could you leverage your support team and delegate more projects to free up your selling time?
- Could you prospect better?
- Could your presentations be better?
- Could you do a better job retaining your clients?
- Could you educate your client on all of your company offerings?
- Could you do a better job owning the objections?
- Could you find a way to set new client meetings?

"Excellence is not a destination; it is a continuous journey that never ends."
—Brian Tracy

Chapter 10

ATTITUDE, APPROACH, ACTION

— — —

Selling is the core of business, and without it some businesses wouldn't exist, so having the right attitude, approach, and action is imperative. These characteristics set the foundation to having a successful sales call, interaction with potential new client, and action required to earn business. It takes attitude, approach, and action working together to make a real impact. You could have a great attitude and approach, but if you lack action you may fall short of your outcomes. Conversely, you could have a great attitude and action but implement the wrong approach to the client. Understanding and embracing all three A's will pay big dividends in the end for you.

Let's review the meaning of attitude, approach, and action.

1. **Attitude:** Your attitude is the way you feel and think.

2. **Approach:** How do you approach each situation?

3. **Action:** What effort and action will you implement? You may have a great attitude and a great approach, but without action nothing comes to fruition.

Our company was introducing a new technology tool so the sales team would have a place to go regarding their accounts. They would be able to access all the data on their accounts in one place. The data that this software provides would allow the salespeople to view their current billing vs. budget, historical information on each of their accounts, pending business, account receivables, invoices, contracts, calendar of appointments, updated account list, and a customer retention program so they could track each interaction. Accessible with a smart phone, it was a very powerful tool at the fingertips of the salesperson.

I encountered some resistance from one of my sellers. I noticed he was not using the tool to its fullest potential. He actually liked writing everything down on his legal pad with his No. 2 pencil. In our weekly one-on-one I asked him what was stopping him from taking advantage of this amazing software. He replied that the system he was using was working for him and had for more than fifteen years. I explained to him that this tool would save him time and could make him more money if he would be open to using it. I made a bet with him that if after ninety days he didn't see an improvement in his business, he wouldn't have to use it. He could return to the legal pad and pencil. He had to commit to using it to the fullest.

What he discovered was that he needed to start with the right attitude, one that he would be willing to embrace as a benefit to himself and his clients. He approached the new program by taking advantage of the help line to educate himself on how to use it to the fullest. Finally, he needed to use the software on a daily basis.

He fulfilled his ninety-day commitment and was so thrilled with the tool that he threw all his legal pads and pencils into the garbage. He became more efficient and in doing so and found a way to create more time with clients.

For You and Your Team

1. **Attitude:** What is your viewpoint, your outlook, your perspective, and stance on how you approach your business? Do you see the world with possibilities or do you quit before you start? Is your energy high or low? Are you eager to meet with new clients or do you hide by staying busy with tasks that don't move your business forward?

2. **Approach:** What are your processes? What are you doing to get closer to your outcomes? What process will you use to get that meaningful meeting? What techniques will you to use to renew a current client? What methods will you put in place to grow your business? How will you solve your client's biggest pain point?

3. **Action:** What massive action must be taken to achieve your outcome? Which strategies will you implement to help solve your client's biggest issues? How much effort will you give each day? What changes must you make? Attitude is everything as long as you have the right approach and take the right action.

Chapter 11

ASK ANOTHER QUESTION

— — —

Has asking questions become a thing of the past? Are we making assumptions on what our client is trying to communicate to us? Have we lost the art of asking better questions when meeting with our team and clients? There are benefits to asking questions. When we ask questions it keeps our team and clients more engaged. By asking additional questions, we can get clarity on what others are trying to communicate to us. The questions we ask guide us to fulfilling their needs and help us discover the biggest challenges they are facing. I found asking more questions helps me gain a better understanding of what others are trying to communicate. I have experienced that the more prepared I am with questions prior to my meeting, the more effective the outcome of the call. I was on a sales call with a client, the owner of a car dealership, who was not currently doing business with us. I asked if he was happy with his sales for the month, and he said he could always do more. I asked how he could grow his market share, and he replied that selling twenty more vehicles would really help. When I asked if there was an opportunity to grow revenue in his service department, he said he was always looking to improve his business in that area. I asked what it would mean to him and his dealership if he could improve his margins by 10 percent, and he replied that the increase would really make an impact on his cash flow. I asked if he would be open to suggestions from our company on creating the opportunity. A week later we provided him with a very thoughtful plan and timelines to accomplish his outcomes, and we won the business! The advantage was that we kept asking questions to see how we could help solve his biggest outcomes.

In today's high-tech world, there's a rush to answer questions quickly. But you must slow down and take the time to ask additional questions so you can make the best possible decisions. You must also encourage your team to ask more questions so they can fully understand what the client's needs are, and then offer a better solution to win the business. You and your team have the opportunity to question your way to a sale.

For You

- Are there questions you should be asking to gain a better understanding of your clients' needs?
- Do you ask probing questions of your team?

For Your Team

Ask your team to share their thoughts on what the phrase "Ask Another Question" means to them.

Next, ask the team to share the best questions they ask on sales calls. Below are examples of three types of questions. Each has a different intent to help you get closer to the real objection.

- **Probing questions** can help uncover the real intent behind what is said: "Can you tell me more?" "Why do you say so?" "What is keeping us from working together?" Many of us don't ask probing questions because we tend to make assumptions and think we understand what the client really means. Effective probing questions help to get the person to talk about their personal opinions and feelings and promote critical thinking.

- **Adjoining questions** are used to explore related aspects of the problem that are ignored in the conversation. Some examples of adjoining questions are "How would that impact your business?" "What else would you need to do to accomplish your outcome?" and "How would these insights change the landscape of your business?"

- **Elevating questions** give us a broader view. Being too immersed in an immediate problem makes it harder to see the overall context behind it. So you can ask, "Let's take a step back; what are the larger issues you are facing?" or "Are we even addressing the right question?"

If we ask better questions, we can expect
better answers!

Chapter 12

BUSINESS OR
BUSYNESS?

Many of us will fall into the busyness trap at some point in our career. Instead of focusing on our business, we look for things that make us feel more accomplished, like cleaning our work space, replying to texts from family or friends, and responding to seemingly endless emails as soon as they arrive. We tell ourselves that after we complete these tasks we'll feel energized and we'll be ready to get back to business.

In a recent *Forbes* article,[4] author Cheryl Conner explored a survey by Salary.com that revealed that the number of people who now admit to wasting time at work every day has reached a whopping 89 percent. A second survey by Harris Poll for CareerBuilder queried hiring managers, HR professionals, and full-time workers across a variety of

---

4   Cheryl Conner, "Wasting Time at Work: The Epidemic Continues," *Forbes*, (July 31, 2015).

industries and company sizes to determine that personal use of technology was a key factor.[5]

According to the survey, time wasters are doing the following:

- 50 percent talk on a cell phone and text.
- 42 percent gossip.
- 39 percent surf the Internet.
- 38 percent spend time on social media.
- 23 percent are distracted by coworker drop-bys.
- 25 percent shop on Amazon.

Respondents said that the number-one reason for slacking was that they didn't feel challenged in their job. Other reasons include working too many hours, being unsatisfied with their career, and being bored. If any of these apply to you, I recommend you evaluate your situation.

I coached one of my account executives to consider finding another career that he might find more fulfilling. I witnessed his enthusiasm dwindle months after accepting the sales position. His father had been ill, and I thought that might have been a contributor. After multiple conversations we discovered that he had always wanted to own his own marketing firm. A free spirit, he wanted the freedom to come and go and call his own shots. I encouraged him to take the time to make certain this is what he wanted. On the following Monday he turned in his resignation. You could see that a weight had been lifted off his shoulders and that

5   Jennifer Grasz, "CareerBuilder Study Revels Top Ten Productivity Killers at Work," *CareerBuilder*, (June 12, 2014).

he had renewed energy. I told him I was proud of him and understood that he needed to do this. He started his own marketing firm and created a successful business for himself.

For You

I encourage you to become more aware of how you spend your time each day. There is a time and place when you will be able to organize your desk and reply to emails and texts from family and friends without taking time away from your work. Decide when and how often you will allow busyness to take away from doing business. My recommendation is to add "busyness tasks" to your calendar each day, allowing for a maximum of twenty minutes in the morning or at the end of the day. Below this entry on your calendar, write "Get back to business!"

Focus and put your energy into growing your business so you can achieve the outcomes you set for yourself. Each of us has the same amount of time each day. The achievers find a way to use their day more effectively.

For Your Team

Ask your team to share their thoughts on what the phrase "Business or Busyness?" means to them.

Next, work with your team to generate a list of "busyness" activities and discuss which action items you may be able to delegate to free up more selling time. For example, you may decide to use your support team to help do your proposals, pull research, collect payment, etc.

If you find yourself looking for busy work vs. business work, break that pattern by getting focused on what needs to be accomplished, or address what may be keeping you from moving forward. Try to be aware of what is shifting you at that moment. You are in control of your destiny.

Chapter 13

IT'S ALL POSSIBLE

— — —

If you want to inspire during a meeting and get others to believe they can achieve anything they set their minds to, then the phrase "It's All Possible!" can help you. Most of us focus on the impossible—that which we are unable to accomplish. But in every impossibility there is possibility. We have the ability to choose either option just by shifting our minds to the outcomes we desire and holding ourselves accountable with an action plan. We get what we focus on. Even the word "impossible" says "I m possible."

Impossible cases are not forever. For example, a seller spent months calling the CEO of a major communications company only to get blocked each time by the gatekeeper, the CEO's assistant. The seller also emailed, tried to connect on LinkedIn, and wrote letters positioning the benefits of meeting. Then it dawned on the seller that most CEOs arrive at the office early, before their support team. She called at 7:00 a.m., and the CEO answered. He was impressed with her determination and agreed to meet with her.

For me, writing this book seemed impossible. I work sixty-hour weeks, sit on several boards, and have a family. I couldn't imagine where I would find the time to write a book. I needed to create a system that would work without taking away from my other responsibilities. I began by creating a strategy to capture my thoughts and devised weekly timelines to hold myself accountable. I created a schedule and dedicated several focused hours on weekends to working through each topic. I found extra hours at night during the week as well. I gave myself a year to complete the process. What seemed impossible became possible for me.

Most people fall short as they give up mentally before they even begin. My advice is to begin and break down how your outcome can fit in your life. While it may seem to be impossible for one salesperson, it might be possible for another. Everything is possible; it's just that the seemingly impossible things take a little longer to figure out. The key is to get your team to understand that figuring it out is a process. Having the internal drive is key, followed by determination to keep pursuing what you want to accomplish.

For You

Identify something you felt was impossible that you made possible. What process did you use to accomplish that project? How do you coach your team through the process of believing everything is possible?

For Your Team

Ask your team to share their thoughts on what the phrase "It's All Possible" means to them.

Recall a time when you created a solution for a situation that seemed impossible. Share the process you went through with your team and describe how you felt when you accomplished it. Ask your team members to share their stories of overcoming similar situations.

Next, ask the team to come up with a list of people throughout history who transformed the seemingly impossible to the possible. Following is a list from biographyonline.net of inventors who made the things we take for granted today possible:

- Thomas Edison developed a wide range of products, from the electric light bulb and the phonograph to motion pictures and the world's first industrial research laboratory.

- The Wright brothers successfully designed, built, and flew the first powered aircraft.

- Benjamin Franklin discovered electricity.

- Alexander Bell invented the first telephone.

- Martin Cooper, a Motorola researcher and executive, created the first mobile phone.

- Henry Ford improved the assembly line for automobile manufacturing and created the Model T, the first gas-powered car.

- Tim Berners Lee developed the http:// protocol for the Internet, transforming and making the World Wide Web freely available.

- Larry Page and Sergey Brin invented Google.

Remind your team that they too have the ability to achieve great outcomes. Encourage them to keep trying new ways until they discover a solution. The journey is part of the learning experience.

"It always seems impossible until it's done."

—*Nelson Mandela*

Chapter 14

OWN THE
OBJECTION

— — —

The sales teams that consistently exceed expectations tend to be more aware of what could keep them from doing business. They are prepared for any objection that their client may present to them. They find a way to build trust with their clients and shift their clients' thinking. They ask clients to have an open mind to the information that they feel confident can help their customer. Most of us buy on emotion and back it up with logic, and so do your clients. The most successful team members are those who emotionally give their clients the benefits of doing business with them and their company.

Most clients want to know they received a fair price and value, so most of us will face the price objection at some point in our careers. Price is an easy objection for the client to position. I see an objection as an opportunity. When a client objects to a price, you have an opportunity to educate and give more information. You have that moment to discuss the cost and the benefits your product can offer them. Perhaps they are still not convinced to move forward. Could there be a hidden objection?

When I recommended a marketing program for a larger automotive client, I put the investment page first in the proposal. He seemed surprised, so I explained that I thought it was important for him to see the investment first and then on the following pages discover what investment it would take to achieve the outcomes we discussed. Those pages included a reminder of the outcome my client desired, which was selling a specific amount of new cars in the month. The program I recommended detailed the strategy and timelines needed to achieve his goals.

Your relationship and ability to think like your client is key. You gain a tremendous advantage over your competition when you're able to eliminate or navigate their objections.

For You

How do you prepare yourself and your team to master the objections? Think like the client. What could arise during your meeting or presentation? Do your research so that you're ready and have the confidence and enthusiasm to lead your team through the process. What do you imagine are the top three objections your team will face during their meetings? How would you overcome these objections? Be prepared to share with your team how you might reply to those objections.

For Your Team

Ask your team to share their thoughts on what the phrase "Own the Objection" means to them.

Next, ask how they would reply to the following objections:

- I am too busy to meet.
- We don't have the budget.
- We are happy with our current provider.
- Send me the information to review.

Next, ask your team for the top three objections they face during their meetings. How might they answer those objections? Be prepared to share with them how you might answer the objections. Once you have agreed on the top three objections and the best verbiage to overcome the objection, have your team learn how to respond to those objections. In the following meeting, ask each team member to answer the objections. A fun way would be to create an objection wheel that is divided into segments, each containing one of the top objections. Have each team member spin the wheel, and then answer the objection that the pointer lands on. When they answer the objection on the spot in front of their peers, they will build confidence and have the ability to answer similar objections when on calls.

Your ability to understand what is prohibiting you from doing business is key. Asking what is keeping you and a client from working together may open up the real reason.

Chapter 15

PROACTIVE OR REACTIVE?

Are you in control of your business, or are you being controlled by your business? Great leaders always have a plan and work it every day with consistency. They don't make excuses for not finding a way. They take a proactive approach to their business every day. They create their way! Let's take a closer look at the meaning of the words "proactivity" and "reactivity."

Proactivity, or proactive behavior, refers to anticipatory, change-oriented, and self-initiated behavior in situations, particularly in the workplace. Proactive behavior involves acting in advance of a future situation rather than just reacting. It means *taking control* and *making things happen* rather than just adjusting to a situation or waiting for something to happen. Proactive employees generally do not need to be asked to act, nor do they require detailed instructions.

I have a client that reaches out to advertise with our company and four or five others every year. As I reviewed the history of the account, I discovered this consistent calling pattern as well as my share of the business. I decided to call them before they called us and to present a creative plan that would garner a larger share of their business. The client was extremely receptive and even stated that I made their job easier by getting ahead of the game. I was able to grow my share by 25 percent, as opposed to the flat or slight increase I received the two years prior.

For You

What can you do about becoming more proactive and less reactive? Create a list of situations in which you find yourself in a more reactive role. Create a list of the productive things you accomplish each day.

For Your Team

Ask everyone to list reactive things they are currently doing today. Have them prioritize, in order, what they react to on a daily or weekly basis. Ask how they can begin to become more aware of their reactive behaviors and shift them to a more proactive approach.

Next, ask everyone to list proactive things they are currently doing. Have them prioritize the items in order of importance.

Follow up with these questions:

- What other ways could you be proactive in your business?

- Have you reached out to clients prior to them calling you?
- Have you shared market research that could impact a client's sales?
- Are you scheduling monthly calls to follow up with current clients?
- Are there other areas of their business where you could provide solutions?

"Either you run your day, or your day runs you."

—*Jim Rohn*

Chapter 16

REASON FOR CALLING

———   ———   ———

Picking up the phone is the fastest way to get on a client's calendar, but too many of us look at the phone as a negative instead of a positive experience. Most of our fear revolves around the potential of being rejected and hung up on. Every great seller has been hung up on. Those who had the courage to push forward likely found all sorts of long-term rewards for the temporary pain they may have experienced when the line went dead.

Here are some points to think about when making calls:

- **In 2007 it took 3.68 attempts to reach the decision maker.** Today it takes 8 attempts.[6]

- **The best times to call** are between 8:00–9:00 a.m. and 4:00–5:00 p.m.[7]

6   TeleNet and Ovation Sales Group, quoted in Wheelhouse Advisors, "How Content Marketing Has Changed the Game," wheelhouseadvisors.net, (Dec. 2, 2014).

7   James B. Oldroyd and David Elkington, "The Lead Response Management Study," leadresponsemanagement.com, (2004–2010).

- **The best days to call** to reach a contact are Wednesdays and Thursdays.[8]

- **Establish a Valid Business Reason (VBR).** Before you reach out to a prospective client, know the VBR for why you are calling. Here is an example of a VBR: "I have key market research on your industry, and it appears that 70 percent of decisions are made by women. Is that the same for you? We should talk. Are you available Tuesday at 9 a.m.?" You will gain more confidence by being prepared with the reason for your call.

- **The value proposition.** How will you benefit the client?

- **Technology is our friend.** Have you done your research? Have you Googled a particular business or industry to discover a reason for calling?

- **Schedule** Have you scheduled on your calendar time to make focused calls? By scheduling the time on your calendar, you will be more in control.

- **The key is your mindset!** Do you approach your calling sessions as "cold calling," which has negative associations, or have you shifted your mindset to "power hour," where you're in control? Is your focus on helping the business owner? Is it your mission to change the landscape of your industry by helping local companies?

- **It starts with the right attitude.** With every rejection, take a moment to capture and analyze the

---

8   Ibid.

situation in order to benefit from the call. You will
view each call as getting better with experience.

- **Develop a professional script** Begin with "Good
  morning, Ms. _____" instead of "Hello." State your
  name and company and why you're calling: "We spe-
  cialize in helping businesses _____." Question
  your way to the appointment: "If we can show you a
  way to improve and save money with a quality product, would you be interested in finding out more?"
  Ask for the meeting by giving them a few options:
  "Would 9:45 a.m. or 3:15 p.m. work for you?"

Have fun calling and connecting to new people that you
and your company can help. Remember, they don't know
what you have to offer them.

I was trying to set an appointment to meet with the
owner of a major insulation company. He was advertising
his product in the market with other radio stations. I knew
advertising on my station could greatly improve his sales.
I had my valid business reason ready prior to picking up
the phone: "My station reaches three hundred thousand
homeowners with a high household income that you're not
currently marketing to. We should talk." I was successful in
scheduling a meeting and converted him to doing business
with our radio station. He appreciated that I called with a
business proposition that could help grow his company.

For You

Identify potential accounts that are not currently doing
business with your company. Take the list of prospects and
divide those accounts across the team. Have them identity the

most important reason for calling. Does your company have appointment-setting scripts for your team to use to create a consistent message when calling on new prospects? Is there an opportunity to practice the script with your team so they gain more confidence prior to making calls? You may consider creating a sales contest and paying a higher commission or bonus for each account converted to an appointment or sale.

For Your Team

Ask your team to share their thoughts on what the phrase "Reason for Calling" means to them. How do they approach their new business calls to secure the meeting?

Next, let's take the list of accounts you identified and shared across the team. Establish with the team one hour a week that everyone agrees to participate in converting the target accounts to appointments. You could title that hour "The Power Hour" or "Treasure Hunting Hour." Each member of the team needs to share with the team what they feel is the reason for calling prior to making the call. Gather the team together five minutes before the call so everyone can focus on what needs to be accomplished. After the hour, have everyone report their results and then discuss and track your progress.

Nobody is too busy. It's just a matter of priorities.

Chapter 17

RAISE YOUR STANDARDS

—— —— ——

Where do you stand? What is the standard of your work? Do you have a high level of quality and excellence, or have you accepted the new normal of average? Think about companies like The Ritz Carlton, Four Seasons, Nordstrom, and Tiffany that raise the standards in their industry.

In the end we are only competing against our own personal best. High performers are focused on becoming better with improved outcomes and their ability to achieve superior results. They determine their high standard. Consider what standard you will accept for yourself. How can you raise your standards?

What traits do high performers have in common? Again and again, it comes down to the same habits, drives, and attitude. They strive to improve through every experience. This high standard of expectation is a way of life for them.

- **Routines.** High performers create routines. They know meeting their high standard will take focused efforts each day. They create processes to look for ways every day to be more effective and efficient. They understand that making small shifts can produce great advantages. Their routines make them highly productive.

- **Will.** They have a strong intention and assertion about their future. They study other high performers to gain knowledge to see if they could implement any of the strategies they have used to improve their performance. Their desire to become the best version of themselves is a way of life.

- **Belief.** They have extreme confidence in themselves.

- **Time.** They understand that raising their standards is a process. There are no shortcuts. It takes time and patience to keep progressing.

Year after year I witnessed one account executive who consistently exceeded her goals. I was astonished to watch her perform at high levels day in and day out. Her success was due to her routines. She came to work at the same time each day (earlier than others) and understood what needed to be completed in that moment and day. If she had a shortfall, she learned from the experience and moved on. She understood the commitment she had to make for herself. I was even more impressed when she stopped to help others on her team. She understood it took time and focused effort, which she was willing to do on a consistent basis.

For You

Do you find yourself going through the motions each day? Where would you describe your standards today? List how you want to change your standards and how you can follow through. Do you believe in yourself? Your team will watch what standard you set for yourself and the company.

For Your Team

Ask your team to share their thoughts on what the phrase "Raise Your Standards" means to them.

Next, ask them to answer these questions:

- What standards do you set for yourself?
- Do you approach your day with your standards in mind?
- Do you believe in your talents?
- Do you have the will to be your very best every day? Do you strive for excellence?

> *"If you want to change your life, you have to raise your standards."*
> —*Tony Robbins*

Chapter 18

THE ONE THING

— — —

"The One Thing" is all about getting your team focused on one thing that could transform their business. In sales we have layers of responsibilities and can lose focus on doing the one thing that can generate more revenue or better results. We always ask our team this question: What is the *one thing* that could change your business?

The one thing that transformed my business was a system I created that included strategic steps and timelines to hold me accountable. I now schedule time on my calendar each week to focus on my priorities. I know if I schedule something that needs to be done, I will do it. I have weekly outcomes for each project to keep me on track to success.

One example of my system at work is finding sales talent for my team. A critical role for leaders is to always be looking for talent to join their teams. Each week I schedule an hour on my calendar titled "Identify Sales Leaders." I review resumes sent to our company, and I prospect on LinkedIn to see people I might be connected with who have the skill sets I'm looking for. I then list my top five targets and begin setting up meetings for current opportunities or for when a position opens.

For You

What is the *one thing* that stands between you and your outcomes? List several things you think could improve your outcomes and choose one you feel could shift your business forward. What could be a difference maker for you?

For Your Team

Ask your team to share their thoughts on what the phrase "The One Thing" means to them. Next, ask your team to take a few minutes to write down several things they think can improve their business. The following examples may help them generate ideas of their own:

- Identifying one more meaningful prospect to call on.
- Having the courage to make one more call.
- Having one more valid business reason for your client to meet with you.
- Having one more meaningful presentation.
- Providing better service and follow-up.
- Learning how to handle the one objection keeping you from closing the deal.
- Asking your best customer for one referral.
- Asking your best customer for an additional order.
- Being more organized.

- Delegating to your support team so you can be in front of more customers.

- Improving your current client relationships.

- Having a positive outlook and more energy throughout the day.

- Having courage to step out of your comfort zone.

Once your team has written down several things they think can improve their outcomes, ask them to pick the one they feel could shift their business forward. The one they feel like doing. The one they plan on doing.

Ask the team to share the one thing they plan to commit to for the next thirty days. Encourage them to track their progress during this time to measure their achievement. (Depending on your sales cycle, you may want to extend the time period of measurement.) Suggest that they print out their one thing and hang it somewhere it is visible to them throughout the day.

Thirty days later, in your sales meeting, review everyone's one thing; discuss the process and celebrate all who achieved their goal. Ask those who fell short to share their one thing and how they approached achieving it the past thirty days. Ask the team to discuss what these team members could have done differently. Encourage those who fell short to be open to the suggestions and then have them implement a new plan and give them weekly outcomes and timelines. Have them again share their experience in thirty days.

Find your one thing and start doing it! You will gain more confidence by achieving the one thing, and it will transform your business. Enjoy the journey!

Chapter 19

LOOKING FOR LEADS

— — —

In sales, leads are the lifelines to our business. The better the leads we discover, the better the opportunity we have to do business with the client. To become a successful salesperson you have to consistently develop prospects on an ongoing basis. How do you find sales leads? Sales leads can come from trade shows, direct marketing, Internet marketing, referrals from satisfied customers, or from cold-calling a prospect.

Most organizations do not have lead-generation programs. In most companies, the sales force generates their own leads. Where can you look for leads from connections you already have? Consider the following connections you may be overlooking:

- Every person you know is connected to about 250 people.

- Life insurance agents are typically connected to 1,200 people.

- Accountants average 300 tax returns a year. They work with business owners to whom you could be introduced.[9]

- Hairdressers and barbers average 200 clients a month.

- Civic organizations allow companies a platform to share how they can help other businesses.

- On average, you'll get one lead from every 10 people you meet at a conference.

- Target online employment sites that are hiring. This is a great indication that their company is expanding and could use your services.

- Articles written about companies are a great lead source, and in various business publications another great lead is when they list employees who have recently been promoted. This is a good opportunity to send a congratulations note to gain access to that decision maker or potential new client.

- Most business owners tend to drive really nice cars. General managers of high-end automotive dealer-ships tend to have amazing relationships with those owners.

- Get to know the owners of high-end restaurants. They cater to business owners and their key clients.

- You have a one-in-two chance of getting more

9   Stephan Schiffman, *Cold Calling Techniques: That Really Work*, (Adams Media Corporation, 2007) 28–31.

business from an existing account. Commit each day to asking for one referral from a satisfied customer.

- Stockbrokers typically have about 200 to 1,000 clients. They may have someone they can refer you to.

- Commercial real estate agents know about companies looking or buying property and expanding into your market. You can start calling on those companies prior to their opening.

- Make a T call. When you go on an appointment, also visit the business on the right, the one on the left, and the one behind your appointment's business. Doing so provides you with three potential prospects.

While having lunch with a friend in the commercial real estate business, my friend told me he was working on finding multiple locations for a new restaurant looking to expand in our market. I asked for more details about the restaurant so I could track down the decision maker at their corporate office. I reached out to their marketing team and was able to put together a program for the grand opening of their stores. I had my program sold before they opened their doors.

For You

- What systems do you have in place that generate leads for your sales team?

- How effective is your team at converting those leads?

For Your Team

Ask your team to share their process in looking for leads.

Next, ask your team how effective they are at converting new business leads. Have them identify three people they can target the following week for new sales leads. It can be from someone you already have a relationship with, like a commercial real estate broker, your insurance provider, or other productive avenues they chose. Have them commit to finding three new business leads and share their experience in the following sales meeting.

It used to be that people needed products to survive.
Now products need people to survive. You're one
lead away from helping that company to connect to
those people who will help their business thrive.

Chapter 20

ARE YOU LISTENING?

— — —

If there is one communication skill you should master, it is the ability to listen. Actively listening can be the key to opening more sales and to providing better customer satisfaction. It can build better relationships with your coworkers and boss.

At times, listening may be difficult for us as salespeople, since we want to solve client problems and we often think we have all the answers. The challenge is focusing on listening. If we are only hearing, we may miss key information our clients are trying to communicate to us. In listening we have the ability to uncover where the real opportunity is to help our clients.

I read an interesting fact—that adults spend an average of 70 percent of their time engaged in some sort of communication. Of this, an average of 45 percent is spent listening, 30 percent speaking, 16 percent reading, and 9 percent writing.[10]

---

10   R. Adler, L. Rosenfeld, and R. Procter, "The Ten Principles of Listening," *skillsyouneed.com*, 2011–2016.

I worked for a boss who was all about time management. He felt that multitasking was a strength and the key to success. Even in meetings he would become very distracted by his mobile device while others were discussing key points. He was hearing what was said, but I wondered if he was actively listening. Although I knew it was not his intention, his distraction broke rapport with the person he was conversing with, which usually caused him to miss the real issue at hand. I learned from that experience, and I now fully focus on what the other person is saying to me. The words people use to communicate give you an opportunity to key in on the message they really want you to receive. Don't get me wrong; it's easy to become distracted by all the messages we receive on a daily basis. But I have more of an awareness now, and my intention on each interaction is to fully listen.

For You

Do you find yourself actively listening, or do you find yourself distracted by other thoughts? Try to remove the distractions and focus on what the other person is saying. Be patient and let the other person take as much time as they need to communicate what they want to say. It's okay to ask clarifying questions once they complete their thoughts if you don't fully understand their point. Start by focusing on what others are communicating to you. I encourage you to take notes to show that you are focused and actively listening. At the end of the day, ask yourself what you learned from the experience.

For Your Team

Ask your team to share their thoughts on what the phrase "Are You Listening?" means to them.

Next, ask the team to spend the entire day just listening! This will take some real focus from them. Ask them to write down what they thought the person in each interaction was trying to communicate to them. Encourage them to be patient and avoid judgment on what is said to them. Ask them to capture the nonverbal communication as well. Have them write down the gestures, facial expressions, and body language of those speaking to see if they align with what the other person is saying. Gather the team at the end of the day to discuss their experiences and what they learned from listening. Was it difficult for them or easy? I have a feeling it may be challenging at first. It will take focus, time, and dedication to shift from talking to listening. It is the one skill to master!

> *"Effective listening is a skill that underpins all positive human relationships. Spend some time thinking about and developing your listening skills; they are the building blocks of success."*
>
> —*Richard Branson*

Chapter 21

WINNING IS CONTAGIOUS

Everyone wants to associate themselves with winners. In business and sales, it's all about stringing together wins. It can begin with a small win, such as picking up the phone and setting a new business meeting or feeding off the energy of a coworker who just closed their first sale. Maybe you asked for a referral from a satisfied client, or maybe you sold a service contract to a current client. I believe that the small wins lead to big wins! You get to experience the energy and excitement you created when you accomplish a goal you set for yourself or your team.

In sports and in business you're competing against other individuals and teams. Everyone does not get a trophy in the business world. Each day someone wins the business, and the other falls short. I believe deep down each of us has a competitive spirit. So how do we make winning contagious? We focus on the wins and find ways to have them each day.

We create an environment that fosters teamwork and creates momentum. Make winning a habit!

Begin by understanding the traits that are common to all people who like to win:

- **Winners believe in themselves.** They have a confident attitude. Great salespeople will always find a way. They look for solutions to clients' needs and, in most cases, deliver on them. They always persevere. Leaders are made; they are not born.

- **Winners influence others.** They have the ability to persuade people in a positive manner and position situations in their favor. This could be convincing the client to buy or gaining a commitment from a potential customer. They have great interpersonal skills. They work to really understand what their customers are saying and communicate in ways that are appropriate to their audience.

- **Winners are team players.** Winning salespeople are collaborators, not combatants. They excel in a culture that supports each other, understanding that each has a role on the team. They learn from their shortfalls and look for ways to improve their performance.

- **Winners are results–oriented.** They are metric-oriented. They are proactive, not reactive. They identify and then act to remove obstacles in their way. They always have a strategy and then follow through on it. This process comes naturally to them. They have mental toughness and a will to win.

I took over as sales manager at a company where year-over-year sales revenue was consistently flat and the attitude of the sales department was status quo with no desire to produce higher results. I was brought in to change that course, and my first order of business was to bring into the group a winning attitude and a vision to succeed. I focused extra attention on the newest rep and coached her to break out of the norm, which she did. Her sales quickly picked up, and she became more confident. Not liking the fact that they were being shown up by someone with less experience, the veterans began to put forth extra effort, and they saw their sales numbers increase as well. Year one produced a 10 percent growth in sales revenue, but years two, three, and four experienced 20 percent growth year over year. Once one person caught the "winning" attitude, it spread throughout the rest of the sales staff. Winning every day became a way of life!

For You

- How do you create a winning environment?
- What level of energy do you bring to the office every day?
- Is there someone on your team you can coach to help energize the rest of the team?
- How do you get each member of your team to commit to winning every day?
- Which sales created the biggest wins and why?
- How will you make it a habit to win every day?

For Your Team

Ask your team to share their thoughts on what the phrase "Winning Is Contagious" means to them.

Next, ask your team these questions:

- How do you mentally approach your day?
- Do you believe in yourself and your abilities to be the best?
- What can you do to get better each day?
- Write down the one sale you're proudest of, and why.
- How do you create a habit of winning?

"Winning means you're willing to go longer, work harder, and give more than anyone else."
—*Vince Lombardi*

Chapter 22

WHAT YOU WANT

— — —

We all have a desire for something. Like most things in life, you get what you focus on. We also need to be clear when meeting with clients what outcomes we expect and the effort and action we are willing to give toward those outcomes. Our mindset is a critical component in getting what we want.

I once had a very inspiring manager who would ask me one question when coaching me before I went on a sales call: What is the outcome that you are looking to achieve with this call? If you know clearly the outcome you are looking to achieve *before* starting the call, you will not allow yourself to leave the appointment before addressing the final goal. So many times we leave thinking we had a "good" meeting, until we realize we did not address the issues related to gaining the desired outcome.

Mastering sales can provide the income of your dreams. The sales process involves strategy, skill, and consistent efforts. It also requires you to make fast, accurate assessments during each interaction. The sales process takes dedication and focus. More importantly, it takes your belief in your heart and yourself.

For You

Next time you are trying to close a new account, ask yourself why it so important for you to do business with that particular client. What would it mean to your business if you were able to close the account? When you become clearer on your outcomes, it helps you remain focused on what actions you need to accomplish.

I recommend the following to keep you focused on achieving your outcomes.

- **Determine what you want.** Be clear as to what you really want. Capture what you want on paper, as it needs to be something you can visualize each day.
- **Ask why you want it.** What is the emotional reason it's a must for you to have?
- **Take action.** What actionable things will you need to do to get what you want?
- **Create a timeline.** How much time will you allow yourself to achieve it? Once you have determined the amount of time, break it down to daily or weekly action items.
- **Celebrate.** Celebrate your accomplishment.
- **Grow.** Now create the next accomplishment you hope to achieve.

For Your Team

Ask your team to share their thoughts on what the phrase "What You Want" means to them.

Next, guide them through the same steps you took in the "For You" section. This process should be used with every account you manage.

You don't get what you want.
You get what you work for.

Chapter 23

WHO KNOWS YOU?

— — —

Most of us in sales have used the question "Who do you know?" as an opportunity to get an introduction to a decision maker. It's also used to gain knowledge or to get one step closer to gaining a place on a client's calendar.

Most people ask something similar when making large purchases or when in need of a service. We ask others about their experience with a particular restaurant, car they own, where we should travel, doctors they recommend, etc. When we do this, we are trying to create some advantage before making a decision about where we should spend our money. This way we feel we are getting a better deal and doing business with people we have more trust with.

But our phrase in this chapter is not "Who do you know?" It's "Who knows you?" Do people know you and your company? To get others to know you takes a focused strategy. Technology has opened the door to you in connecting to those in your city, state, country, and the world. If you're thought of first in your industry, you have the competitive advantage.

Below is a list of recommendations on how to leverage technology to market yourself so that more people will find out about you. You would be surprised how many don't take advantage of social media.

- **LinkedIn.** LinkedIn is the hub of online professional networking. You can showcase problems you've solved in your industry; convert your goals into keywords to include in your profile; build your connections; and get endorsements to establish credibility.

- **Twitter.** Twitter is a quick way to efficiently disperse short messages. You want to produce professional content to position you and your brand or services specifically.

- **Pinterest.** Pinterest is your visual website. It is ideal for marketing a creative, visually stimulating service like food industry, construction, or interior design.

- **YouTube.** Everyone can take advantage of YouTube. You can post instructional videos for your products and interviews with employees or satisfied customers.

- **Blog.** A personal blog or company blog is an integral part of marketing yourself. You can really position yourself by having that online presence, because it allows you to create your own content. You can have current and new prospects follow your updates on your company or you personally. Industry standards recommend two blog posts per week, which will help your SEO ranking in Google. Include photos, and keep your posts under a thousand words.

- **Email marketing**. This is a great way to communicate on a monthly basis.
- **Video referrals**. Have your current clients make short videos recommending you, which you can send to prospective clients.
- **Networking**. Join groups that connect with your industry. Take advantage of those meeting by interacting with as many people as possible. Be vocal at those meetings so people know who you are.

For You

Brainstorm a list of ways you can get others in your industry and potential clients to notice you.

For Your Team

After you've brainstormed your list of ways to get others in your industry and potential clients to notice you, share it with the team. Ask them to build on it by brainstorming other possibilities.

The best way to grow your business is to have the client think of you first!

Chapter 24

BEGIN AND WIN

— — —

Traditionally, the beginning of the New Year is the time we set goals and objectives for what we want to accomplish before the next year rolls around. We begin with focused energy and great intentions. But why wait until New Year's Day? You can set out on a winning path right this minute. The most challenging part is getting started. What have you been putting off that could change your business outcomes? Realize that if you don't begin, you miss the opportunity to win.

My boss wanted to help me generate leads to target. One of the leads was a pizza chain. They were known to do business with our competitors as well as other media outlets. My regular effort of cold-calling found that the pizza chain was comprised of a group of franchisees. My fear was that I was going have to spend the time forming a "relationship" with each franchisee and securing their recommendation on the next annual marketing summit. Instead of getting overwhelmed by the task at hand, I formulated a plan to tackle the biggest franchise owner, and get his/her recommendation as well as direction on whom to go to next. With this approach, taking one franchise owner at a time, the biggest to the smallest, I was able to secure an invitation to their marketing summit to submit a plan that was signed off on by the individual owners, and I ultimately earned their business.

For You

I have outlined some tips and trends to consider that will help you begin.

- **Reflect.** Take the time to review where you are today. Have you met your goals? Are you satisfied with the outcomes? Answering these questions will help you determine what you need to focus on to win.

- **Create a roadmap.** List three things that describe where you are right now. Now list the three things that describe where you want to be next month, then in six months, and then next year. Based on where you are and where you want to be, what do you have to do to get there? Your answer is your roadmap! Break it down into achievable sections, assign a completion date to each action item, and begin to win. For example, you may want to set more meaningful meetings with prospective clients. You review where you currently are with setting those meetings. Your records show you set one per month. Your outcome is to set three per month. So you begin identifying what the meaningful meetings have in common. Does the client have the resources to do business with you?

Your roadmap outcome is that you have decided to schedule "power hours" to set new business calls. You will do this on Tuesdays at 3:00 p.m. and Fridays at 9:00 a.m. You will add hours each week until you have achieved setting your three new client meetings.

- **Measure it.** What gets measured gets done. Measuring your goals on a regular basis will not only hold you accountable, it will also ensure that they are feasible. In addition, consistent tracking allows you to see your progression to determine whether or not you're on track. You have a visible roadmap that allows you to reevaluate and take different roads if necessary. Monitoring your outcomes will assist you in prioritizing so that you can focus your resources and time on the outcomes that will make the biggest impact for you.

- **Celebrate.** You want to take the time to celebrate that you began something with a very specific outcome. You should also take the time to recognize what you experienced and learned along the way.

For Your Team

Ask your team to share their thoughts on what the phrase "Begin and Win" means to them.

Next, ask how many of them have created a New Year's resolution. What were the outcomes from those resolutions? Did they accomplish those outcomes? If they fell short of their outcomes, what did they learn about themselves? Finally, walk them through the process of reflecting and creating a roadmap. Discuss how they should measure their goals on an ongoing basis. Don't forget to celebrate with them for beginning something with a very specific outcome.

"Winning is not everything, but the effort to win is."

—*Zig Ziglar*

Chapter 25

ONE MORE CALL

— — —

We ask that each team member bring the following to our "One More Call" meetings: total revenue they generated, their total number of accounts, and their current compensation plan. We then share the following example with them to show how they could use these numbers to determine the impact making one more call can have on their income. Kim, a commission sales person for the ABC Company, generated $900,000 in revenue over the year for ABC from her ten accounts. The average account she is responsible for represents $90,000. The current commission plan is 10 percent. Therefore, every account is worth $9,000 in commissions to Kim.

Kim knows what it means to make one more call. One more call leads to one more appointment. Appointments lead to prospects, which lead to sales. The next step for Kim will be figuring out what to do with an extra $9,000.

By adding one more call to your day, you get more sales opportunities. One more call every day for a five-day workweek is approximately 250 more calls per year. If your closing average is 20 percent, that equates to fifty more sales per year (more than four per month depending on your industries sales cycle) simply by adding one more call.

Note: Depending on your company's sales cycle and compensation, you may need to adjust this exercise. If your team is not paid on full commission, you may shift the focus of the meeting to how important it is for your team to retain customers or how important service is to every account.

For You

Figuring out your team's numbers prior to the meeting and then creating checks with their names and dollar amounts on them can help drive home your point of making one more call. Customize each check using phrasing similar to "One More Call, $9,000 payable to Kim Smith." Put the checks in an envelope and hand them out to your team in the meeting once you have them complete the exercise below. Salespeople tend to be visual, so showing them what their efforts can create will inspire them and keep them focused. You may take it a step further and ask them how they would spend the money.

For Your Team

Ask your team to share their thoughts on what the phrase "One More Call" means to them.

My team loved discovering how much they could make in commissions, and they saw the importance of making one more call each day. Guide your team through the exercise using the team's collective revenue so that they each understand their individual impact on the revenue.

Making one more call keeps your business growing
and you in control of your destiny!

Chapter 26

THE SMART
APPROACH

— — —

Success is not some distant external goal. Success comes from learning through your own experiences and the experiences of others. Along the way you gain knowledge, which will allow you to make smarter decisions and develop a better approach.

By using the acronym SMART you are able to reach your goals and objectives while holding yourself accountable.

- S—strategy. What is your vision for your business?

- M—measure. How will you track your progress?

- A—action. What action is needed to achieve your outcomes?

- R—results. What results are you expecting?

- T—timeline. What is your timeline for completing your outcomes?

During lunch with a realtor friend, I asked how many houses she had sold. She said she'd sold twelve that year, but she would love to sell even more. I asked her what system she was using to help grow her business, and she shared that she was relying on friends, family, and referrals for leads. I explained how each step of the SMART approach could transform her business:

S: I asked her to dream big and tell me how many houses in a year would get her really excited. She said selling fifty houses would stretch her, but would earn her a six-figure income.

M: I asked how she could measure her activity to help her sell the number of homes she wanted to sell. She knew she needed to find a way to connect to more potential home buyers. She had been meeting with about ten to twelve prospects per month. She would need to increase her leads fivefold.

A: She made an agreement with herself to contact and meet with twenty prospects per week. Over the month she would have created eighty prospects.

R: She would start to record her progress by tracking the number of calls she made each week, keeping in mind that one hundred per month was her goal. If she fell short one week, she would make up those calls the next week. She understood the importance of the leads, as they represented her road to making more income.

T: She committed to setting timelines to ensure she stayed on track in what she needed to accomplish on a daily, weekly, and monthly basis.

I kept in touch with her to see how she progressed using the SMART approach. She loved the system and sold forty-five homes, which was five shy of her goal. She was excited about her accomplishment and looked forward to exceeding her personal best year the following year.

For You

Are there opportunities to implement the SMART approach to help improve your and your team's performance? Think about the questions below and how they can improve your team's performance.

- Strategy: What is the team's strategy?
- Measure: How will you measure your team's progress?
- Action: What actions and approach are needed to accomplish the outcomes?
- Realistic: Have you set realistic goals for your team to achieve?
- Timeline: What is your timeline for completing this project?

For Your Team

Ask your team to think about their business and apply the SMART approach by having them answer the following questions.

- Strategy: What is your vision for your business?
- Measure: How will you track your progress?
- Action: What action is needed to achieve your outcomes?

- Results: What results are you expecting?
- Timeline: What is your timeline for completing your outcomes?

"To design the future effectively, you must first let go of your past."
—*Charles J. Givens*

Chapter 27

MAKE MEETINGS MEANINGFUL

In most cases it takes time to get in front of a decision maker and have her schedule you on her calendar. Therefore, you want to create the best first impression possible so you can have future meetings. The question is, how do you take advantage of the time and make certain your meeting has meaning?

The good news is that you, as a leader, set the tone of the meeting. You must be prepared and commit to the time it takes to make that meeting memorable. Forget about showing up and winging it.

During a discussion with a new salesperson before her first call meeting, I asked her to share the questions she had prepared for the call. I could tell by her response that she was not as prepared as she could be and was going to wing it. When asked how many times she had reached out to the potential client, she replied that she had made twenty various attempts before securing the meeting. "You invested a lot of time to get this appointment," I said, "and you're going on the call unprepared?" She apologized and said she was glad we were having this conversation. I also reminded her of what the client's first impression may be of her if she was unprepared. We then discussed more thoughtful questions she could ask. We role-played the call so she could be as prepared as possible.

When she made the call, she had more confidence than she had before our discussion, and the client was impressed. He even shared with her how most salespeople come in and waste his time. Instead, he found their interaction very beneficial. Investing value time upfront to prepare for your meeting can result in a more productive call. The preparation should help you build confidence, produce more knowledge about your client, and gain their respect for understanding how you value their time.

For You

Below are strategies that will help you be prepared for your next team meeting.

- **Determine the outcome you want to accomplish.** The agenda of the meeting should be focused on the outcome you want to accomplish. Often we go into a meeting unprepared or include too many messages.

- **Communicate the outcome you want.** You must understand the importance of conveying the message to your team. Communicating the outcome you want from your team is critical. You will need to be prepared and know what you want to say and how you will present it prior to meeting with your client.

- **Practice makes perfect.** Spend the time reviewing and practicing your meeting. Think about how your team will react to your message. My recommendation is to take the time upfront, as it will likely pay big dividends in the end.

- **Be prepared.** You are more likely to gain respect from your team if you come prepared. They will understand that you value their time as well as your own. Believe in yourself as you put the necessary time into this meeting.

- **Be confident.** Make certain you show up early to the meeting and create the winning mindset. Being prepared and practicing before the meeting will have you confidently accomplishing your outcome.

- **Have fun.** You have invested your time and energy preparing for the meeting, so enjoy the journey. You will walk away learning something from the meeting. Celebrate your efforts!

For Your Team

Ask your team how they can make their meetings more meaningful. Next, have the team share their favorite meeting and why they felt that meeting was successful.

Below are strategies to discuss with your team that will help them be prepared for their next meeting.

- **Determine the outcome you want to accomplish.**
  The agenda of the meeting should be focused on the outcome you want to accomplish. Often we go into a meeting unprepared and as a result miss the opportunity to achieve our desired outcome.

- **Communicate the outcome you want.** You must understand the importance of conveying the message you want to get from the client. For example, in sales our outcome is to sell our goods or services to the client. Communicating the benefits we offer is critical. You will need to be prepared and know what you want to say and how you will present it prior to meeting with your client.

- **Practice makes perfect.** Spend the time practicing your call with others in your building. Explain the outcome you want to achieve. Ask for objections or pushback so you can be prepared. This will allow you to perfect your call or presentation so it comes across seamlessly. My recommendation is to take the time upfront, as it will likely pay big dividends in the end.

- **Be prepared.** You are more likely to gain respect from the customer if you come prepared. Doing so will convey that you value their time as well as your own. Believe in yourself as you put the necessary work to make this call successful!

- **Be confident.** Make certain you show up early to the meeting and create the winning mindset. Being prepared and practicing before the meeting will have you confidently accomplishing your outcome.

- **Have fun.** You have invested your time and energy preparing for the meeting. Enjoy the journey! You will walk away learning something from the call. Celebrate your efforts!

"Luck is a matter of preparation meeting opportunity."
—*Oprah Winfrey*

Chapter 28

ARE WE PREPARED?

— — —

One of the most important steps in the sales process is being prepared. We are given one opportunity to impress and earn the client's trust based on how prepared we are for the call. Our focus is to discover how we can recommend solutions to their biggest problem. In order to do so we must be prepared prior to our first meeting. This is a process and takes a commitment from you. We have invested valuable time in prospecting the client and need to make certain we don't end up unprepared for the call rather than investing the necessary time upfront to be the most prepared we can be. In doing so you will be viewed as more of a resource to them and their company.

Below are three strategies that will guide you to have a more productive call by being more prepared.

1. **Know your outcome.** You want to know the outcome you want to accomplish in the meeting. This is the most fundamental step of the sales process. The truth is

that most of us miss this critical step. We are so grateful we set the meeting that we tend to move on and don't identify a clear expectation. Using your time wisely will pay off big dividends.

2. **Do your research.** Once you know the outcome you want to accomplish, it's critical to be as prepared as possible. You can prepare by gathering information through many sources, including:

   a. The company will typically have press releases, awards, and information about community involvement and the company structure on its website.

   b. Google the industry to discover any trends or new product launches.

   c. Try to discover which provider they are currently using and the advantages and shortfalls that company may have.

   d. Find out who the key decision makers are who have the power to approve your proposal.

   e. How are timelines established?

   f. Contact the top salesperson at the company and offer to buy them lunch or coffee. They can give you their insight on what the company's current outcomes or challenges may be prior to your meeting.

3. **Practice makes perfect.** This is a critical step, and your practice needs to be more than you reviewing the questions or proposal in your mind. You will build credibility in the prospect's eye by doing your research and having thought-provoking questions.

The more prepared you are, the more confident you will be and the greater success you will achieve! I had a salesperson who had been prospecting an automotive client who was doing business with a competitor. She had stayed relevant over the year by sending articles and following up with quarterly calls. She understood that she would have a chance to earn the business when they started accepting proposals for the following year. The time came and she secured her appointment with the client and advertising agency. She discovered an opportunity for the client to reach the female car buyer. She had done her homework and knew the other media outlets the client had been purchasing didn't have the ability to deliver the female consumer. She was prepared with a thoughtful and strategic program to expand their marketing and sales message.

The first page of the proposal was focused solely on the client and the benefits to them by adding our radio station. She included the investment page near the front of the proposal instead of at the end. She wanted to show the return on investment the client could expect when purchasing her station while maintaining their current media partners. The client was extremely impressed by how prepared she was for the meeting. She knew about the client, the company needs, and how to position the value of adding her station and the impact that could have on their revenue. The way she approached this client became the new normal for her. Her business continues to flourish, and her client referrals have grown immensely.

For You

Do you have a process that your team follows so they are prepared for each call? Share an example of a call where you fell short of expectation due to not being as prepared as possible. Share an example of a call where you were prepared and successful in earning the business.

For Your Team

Ask your team to share their thoughts on what the phrase "Are We Prepared" means to them.

Next ask your team how they prepare for each call or meeting. Have your team share an example of a call where they were prepared and how the client felt about their meeting.

Have them write down one client they are not currently doing business with. Spend time creating a well-thought-out plan including the benefits your company has to offer the client. Is there additional research or trends that can be added to your strategy to make the call as effective and impactful as possible? Present all your ideas to the team to see if they can add contributions that could enhance the call.

Plan, prepare, perform!

Chapter 29

OWN YOUR NUMBERS

— — —

In sales, "owning your numbers" means taking personal responsibility for hitting or, better yet, exceeding your sales goals for the year. What strategy do you implement to make certain you exceed your goals? With an annual budget, for example, of $2 million in sales, with a 12 percent increase over the prior year, you may think there would be no way to achieve that budget. To make the number seem more manageable in our minds, we would need to first break it down. I needed to do this with my budget, $1 million in revenue, which represented a 5 percent increase over the prior year. In order to achieve that goal, I needed to make certain that I retained my base accounts, which represented $800,000 in revenue. I strategized by offering additional services to my current base of accounts, which represented another $80,000 in revenue. My next goal was to create $120,000 in new business in order to achieve my budget. This is where the fun began. I broke down the number to $12,000 per month in new clients. I was able to identify twelve key targets that I could approach with solutions to their marketing. I was determined to gain one new client a month, and I knew that doing so would help me exceed my budget. When I closed each sale I took the time to celebrate that I was one step closer to achieving my goal.

For You

These three steps will keep you focused on what you need to do in order to achieve your goals.

Step One: Owning Your Number

To own your number, you must first determine what that number is. Is it a monthly, quarterly, or annual goal? You need to take full responsibility for your budgets. Do you have a strong will and winning attitude when approaching your goals?

Step Two: Strategies to Achieving Your Number

Will you need focused time to set up new meetings with customers? Will you need to find a way to expand your customer base? Will you need to get your current customers to spend more with you? Can you create a way to get your average sale increased? Will you delegate by leveraging all non-selling items to your support team? Will you ask for a referral from a satisfied customer? Will you expect more from yourself daily? Will you measure your progress? Focus your time and energy on items that produce results.

Step Three: Celebrate Exceeding Your Number

Take the time to celebrate once you have achieved your number! We live in a fast-paced world and need to take the time to reflect on our successes. I would recommend writing down that success—the business you closed and the process it took to win that business. This will give you confidence as it shows you've already been there. If you fell short, then you can learn from those experiences as well. What would you do differently next time?

For Your Team

Ask your team to share their thoughts on what the phrase "Own Your Number" means to them.

Next, lead them through the three-step exercise posed earlier.

"The difference between a successful person and others is not a lack of knowledge, but rather a lack of will."

—*Vince Lombardi*

Chapter 30

I WILL KNOW

———   ——   ——

It's vital in sales to understand your clients' businesses and know how you can help solve their biggest outcomes. The Internet provides us an opportunity to research the industry, the client, and the contact we are meeting with. We are able to gather enough knowledge prior to our call. The extra time you invest upfront will pay off big dividends in the end. The phrase "I Will Know" is a commitment made by you to really understand the needs of your clients.

We have a choice when we don't fully know something. We can ignore it and agree it's okay not to know the answer or have more information at that moment. Or we can expand ourselves by learning something new. We understand that all clients have different expectations and needs from us. If we can identify those needs, we have a major advantage over our competition. The more we know about a situation, the better solutions we can provide to our clients and customers. I encourage you to make a commitment to knowing more than anyone else about your client. It's the key to winning their trust and business.

One of my salespeople was having difficulty finding a business reason to meet with a client. He researched on the Internet as much as he could about the company and what services they provided. He knew everything from their mission statement to all their community involvements, but he needed to find a way to see where his opportunities were prior to calling. We thought if we could find a way to meet with the top salesperson at the organization, they would be the key to understanding the company's biggest challenges and give us a better opportunity to understand where we could help.

We invited the top seller of the company to lunch. We gained so much knowledge about the company, the challenges they were facing, who they were currently doing business with, who had the authority to make purchasing decisions, and the possible solutions we could provide. We gathered knowledge and gained the confidence to set the meeting, and then we met with the client, who was extremely impressed with our thoughtful questions and understanding of his desired needs, sales cycle, and timelines. We earned his business due to our commitment of knowing more than our competition.

For You

- List your company's top thirty accounts and write down what you know about those clients, including who can say yes to your proposal.

- List your top ten accounts that you see as providing the biggest opportunities for doing business with and write down what you know about each client.
- Create a strategy for each account to win their business.

For Your Team

Ask your team to share their thoughts on what the phrase "I Will Know" means to them.

Next, ask each person to list one client they are currently doing business with and one client they are targeting to earn their business. Have them write down the answers to the following questions for both clients:

- Do I know the decision makers?
- What are my clients' outcomes?
- What are my clients' timelines?
- What moves my clients emotionally?
- What are my company's competitive advantages?
- Why did they choose the competition over us?
- Do they have the budget to accomplish their outcomes?
- Do I understand their industry advantages?
- Can I present strategies to solve my clients' biggest issues?
- Do I know my clients' sales cycles?

- Can I answer why we are not currently doing business together?

The ability to ask more questions until you have enough knowledge about your clients' needs is the key to doing business with them.

"Knowledge isn't power until it is applied."

—*Dale Carnegie*

Chapter 31

WIN THE DAY

— — —

How do you create a productive week, month, and year? You start with focusing on one day at a time. The equalizer is that each of us has the same 1,440 minutes each day. How productive we are will depend on how we spend those minutes. We have the opportunity to create small wins, which can turn into big days. How will you take advantage of your day? To successfully manage your time and grow your business, you need to ask yourself the question: Does this activity advance my business?

Here are five thought-starters to help you create winning days: **I can't do everything today, but I can get started on one thing.** You have plans, and you have goals to achieve. But you have nothing until you actually do something. Pick one plan, one goal, or one idea, and get started. The first step is by far the hardest.

1. **I will do one thing others are not willing to do.** Be willing to do what others think about or refuse to do. Find one

thing other people won't do. It can be small. Whatever it is, do it. You'll be doing it while others are watching. Make it a ritual to do one thing each day that others may be afraid to start. After a period of time, you will develop determination and willpower.

2. **Get out of your comfort zone.** Fear is the most common trait that stops us. Commit to doing something that will stretch you out of your comfort zone. You will gain confidence from the experience and realize that the scenario you created in your mind was less scary than it turned out to be.

3. **Two ears, one mouth.** Make it a point to listen twice as long as you would talk. You'll be amazed how much more you can learn from just listening.

4. **Out-hustle everyone.** Start your day knowing that it's your *will*, not necessarily your *skill*, that can make a major impact on your day. Approach your day with a strategy of what must get completed versus a wish list of items you hope to accomplish. Be strategic when you schedule your meetings outside the office so you won't be wasting valuable minutes driving all over town or sitting in traffic.

As a new manager, I realized that my days were filled with activities that were not producing the best outcomes. I decided to track each day to see how I was spending my time. I discovered that I needed a better approach to my day in order to achieve the outcomes expected. In my day there were set meetings that I needed to attend and paperwork that needed to be completed and emails and phone calls that needed to be returned. I wanted to create a day with more purpose, which meant meeting with new prospects, current clients, and connecting with my team. I needed to take ownership of my day and not allow the distractions of emails and reports to hinder me from doing so.

The game plan I created for winning the day is as follows: I start my day meeting with my one of my salespeople to review their business needs and see how I can help move their business forward. I schedule a meeting with a new prospect or attend a call with my sales team. This gives me a chance to connect with my salesperson and grow new accounts for our company. Then I schedule a meeting with an existing client currently doing business with us. I focus on our top-spending clients who generate the most revenue. Those meetings may be lunches or golf to further build our relationships. I block out time on my calendar to return emails and phone calls, which I prioritize. I find my days are more productive, and I am more focused on creating better results for my business.

For You

- How do you ensure you get the most important outcomes you need each day?

- How do you hold your team accountable to having productive days?

- Are there meaningless tasks stealing valuable time from you moving forward?

- Who on your team should you be spending more time with in order to produce greater results?

- How can you be more efficient?

For Your Team

Ask your team to share their thoughts on what the phrase "Win the Day" means to them.

Next, ask them what rituals they have in place to get the most productivity out of their day. Recommend that they spend a day or workweek tracking each minute. Next to each activity have them put a "P" for productive and "T" to note time waster of an activity that may be costing them sales.

"When you wake up, think about winning the day. Don't worry about a week or a month from now—just think about one day at a time. If you are worried about the mountain in the distance, you might trip over the molehill right in front of you."

—*Drew Brees, quarterback, New Orleans Saints*

Chapter 32

WHAT STOPS YOU?

— — —

What stops you from achieving your goals? If you're not accomplishing your goals or are struggling to reach them as quickly as you want, let's consider what may be prohibiting you:

- **Excuses:** You make excuses for yourself. You need to take care of your emails, talk with the IT department, organize your desk, and talk with coworkers. Ask yourself what tasks can wait until you accomplish the most important task of the day.

- **Waiting for others:** Sometimes your team members or peers don't take the job seriously, which may lead to you taking it less seriously as well. Whose outcome does this diminish? Yours!

- **Waiting for the right time:** The time is now; take action.

- **Multitasking:** It is not possible to multitask and give 100 percent of your attention to each activity.

- **Giving up:** Have you ever given up too quickly out of fear? If you miss the mark at something, learn from it and try again. If you miss the mark again, learn some more and try again. You will always learn something from trying.

- **Not taking risks:** Picking up the phone is inherently risky, but you've made it this far. Take the first step, as the rewards will far outweigh the fear of never having risked at all.

- **Mindset:** Our minds are very powerful. We get to decide how we will approach every situation and how much energy we are willing to put toward it. If you create a can-do attitude and tell yourself that you are going to focus and give 100 percent of your attention, you'll be further than others. This will empower you and help you take control of the situation.

I was coaching a salesman through a major presentation he had to make in front of a large group of decision makers. He had never presented in front of more than a few people. He had always had a fear of public speaking but had managed his anxiety in front of small groups. He realized that he was stopping himself from stepping out of his comfort zone. I shared that one of the biggest fears people have is public speaking. I told him that he would gain a tremendous amount of confidence each time he got in front of others and shared his thoughts. By putting himself in those situations, he would be able to tap into those experiences. It's all about being prepared and shifting your mindset from fear to confidence. Our minds can only focus on one thought at a time.

He prepared his presentation, and I filled the conference

room with other coworkers and had him go through the presentation. I knew he would gain confidence by having to present to his peers. He nailed it! He was successful in his presentation and was eager to do the next one.

For You

- What is one thing stopping you?
- What can you do to overcome what's stopping you?
- Can you identify what may be keeping team members from moving their business forward?
- What recommendations can you offer your team to keep them moving forward?

For Your Team

Ask your team to think about what stops them from moving their business forward. What stops them from setting up new business meetings? What stops them from closing that meaningful client? Once they have identified the one thing holding them back, ask them to develop a game plan on how they could overcome it. What steps would they need to take to gain confidence in moving forward? I recommend coaching them through the process until you feel they have mastered it. The time you spend helping them will pay major dividends.

"The first step toward getting somewhere is to decide that you are not going to stay where you are."

—*John Pierpont Morgan*

Chapter 33

BECAUSE OF YOU

— — —

More than ever, companies are focusing on their culture as a competitive differentiator. They are seeing how cultivating the right culture can engage current employees and recruit new ones while increasing the bottom line. These three words—Because of You—are for employee recognition, employee engagement, and retention. Employee recognition is the acknowledgment of an individual's or team's behavior, effort, and accomplishment that support the organizations goals and values.

Recognition is a key tool in any employee retention program for a reason: People need recognition for their efforts. They need to feel like they are contributing and making a difference for the company. We are moving so fast to hit the monthly, quarterly, and annual budgets that at times we miss the opportunity to pause and celebrate all the contributions from our team and the wins for our company. The daily wins build to a great month, and great months build to an outstanding year. You have the ability to create a winning environment by sharing the team's accomplishments.

At the end of each quarter we meet as a team and review all that we have accomplished and what we still need to achieve as a team. We take the time to celebrate the wins and brainstorm ideas on what we can do to improve where we fell short. The reason we do this each quarter is that it allows us the time to recognize our achievements up to that point, and we have the ability to adjust our strategy for the next quarter. The team understands it's a process that allows us to tap into the company's talent to contribute new concepts that we may need to implement moving forward in order to reach our goals.

You have the ability to create a winning environment where employees feel like they are making a difference. Take the time to understand that the human capital of your company is the key to our success.

For You

- How do you recognize your employees' achievements?

- Identify the achievements of your company on a quarterly basis and recognize those who have contributed over and above expectation.

- Create a platform for employees to share thoughts on how you can improve your metrics moving forward. It could be improving your current systems or a sales idea to generate business for the next quarter.

For You and Your Team

Ask your team to share their thoughts on what the phrase "Because of You" means to them.

Next, identify your team's achievement by finishing the following phrases listed below and share these answers with your team.

- Because of you, we achieved _____.
- Because of you, we can celebrate _____.
- Because of you, we can _____.
- Because of you, our service is the best in the industry.
- Because of you, we acquired more new clients.
- Because of you, we retained X percent of our clients.
- Because of you, we grew our employee count to X.
- Because of you, we grew our shares in the market-place by X.
- Because of you, we exceeded our goals by X.
- Because of you, we beat cash flow by X.
- Because of you, we have a major competitive advantage over our competitors.
- Because of you, we were able to help our community _____. (Insert how your company gives back.)

Coming together is a beginning. Keeping together is progress. Working together is success.

Chapter 34

YOUR SALES STORY

— — —

Everyone on your team has a story. They have a personal-journey story, and they have a work story. We are the authors of our own stories, and chapters get written along the way with each experience. You have the option of sharing your story with others, including your clients. Everyone loves a good story, whether it's an adventure, love story, or one filled with action. One of the most powerful ways to convey your message is by telling a story.

My sales story started in a small town in Wilmington, Ohio, at radio station WSWO and WKFI (We keep farmers informed). I had just graduated from college, and this was my first sales job. I drove an hour each way to work at the radio station, which was in the country. Calling on my first client, Bright Appliances, was an adventure. Bright Appliances was a used furniture store. I was charged with getting them to advertise on our radio station. I walked in and introduced myself to the owner and her Shar-Pei, who was sitting in a recliner. I pulled out my list of questions to gain more knowledge about her needs. Google and the Internet didn't exist in 1988. I gathered all the information I needed, and I secured a second appointment.

I was very excited about the creative concept I thought would have a really big impact on her store. A few days later I went back to Bright Appliances with my first proposal and commercial. I was so excited as I strolled into the store with great confidence. I didn't realize until I got there that I didn't have a cassette player to play the commercial. The woman offered one of her used players to me. The dog was again sitting in the chair, now waiting for the big moment. I hit the Play button, but no sound came out. I was checking the volume when the recorder began eating the tape in the cassette. The owner started yelling at me for breaking her used cassette player. I was devastated. All I could think was, "Four years of college for this?" Back in my car, I nearly cried.

I returned to the radio station to make another copy and then went back to Bright Appliances, this time with the station's cassette player. As she listened to the commercial, the owner grinned, and the dog actually lifted her head. The owner signed the deal. I often think about that first sale and where I am today. What an adventure it has been!

For You

What are you willing to do before your story ends? Write your answers to the following questions:

- What story can you share about your first sale?
- What changes do you need to make right now?
- How will you approach your day differently?

- How do you want to be remembered?
- What impact will you have during your career?
- Will you continue to go through the motions and blend in with others?
- What actions must you do right now to make certain you achieve your happy ending?

For Your Team

Ask your team to share their thoughts on what the phrase "Your Sales Story" means to them.

Next ask them to answer the following questions:

- What story do you share with your clients?
- What story do you tell yourself?
- Are you a solution provider?
- Do you make your clients laugh?
- Do you educate your clients on the benefits of your products?
- Are you the best salesperson in your industry?
- Do you have the best relationships with your clients?
- Do your clients call you first when they need solutions to their business issues?
- Will you get promoted to management?
- Do others on your team follow your lead?

People will remember your stories before they remember your sales pitch.

Chapter 35

FIND A WAY!

— — —

We all encounter difficulties or roadblocks that keep us from achieving our outcomes. But achieving these desired outcomes *is* possible; you just need to find a way. First you must identify what it is you are seeking.

Below are a few suggestions of outcomes that you or your team may be seeking:

- Find a way to acquire new clients.
- Find a way to get more revenue from current clients.
- Find a way to get on your prospects' calendars.
- Find a way to get more client referrals.
- Find a way to exceed revenue expectations.
- Find a way to have better customer service.
- Find a way to hire more sales talent.
- Find a way to build employee morale.

- Find a way to delegate more so you can work *on* your business, not *in* it.

- Find a way to get promoted.

Depending on the size of your company, building a positive work environment and maintaining employee morale may be challenging. Every department plays an important role in the success of the organization. Typically the focus is on the sales organization. How do you recognize those in your organization and let them know they are appreciated?

Our company created a quarterly luncheon off-site for all employees. All departments had the opportunity to connect with each other. We would update everyone on how our division was performing compared with the market, and how we were performing against budget. We also recognized various employees for their leadership or contributions that were over and above expectations. The luncheons created appreciation for the team, and employees would post on social sites how cool our company was, which was great for retention and recruitment.

Everyone wants to know they are making a difference at work. Employees are a great resource for ideas and solutions on what a company may be trying to accomplish and for finding ways to improve overall operation. They just need a platform to share.

Each of us is capable of finding a solution to our outcomes. We may need to try various approaches. We have the opportunity to gain knowledge along the way until we reach our destination. Our desire to achieve more for ourselves is the difference between those who find their way and those still searching.

Here are examples of those who found a way:

- **Lisa, a marathon runner.** You don't just wake up one day and go run 26.2 miles. Most of us have a hard time driving 26.2 miles, let alone running it. Lisa created a seventeen-week program that built miles on each week so she was physically and mentally ready to run the marathon on race day.

- **Steve Jobs.** The creator of Apple Inc., he may be one of the greatest inventors of the last century. He revolutionized the computer by adding his touches, creating the Macintosh. He found a way to make the mouse a better device for communicating with computers. He found a way to tweak and reinvent the iMac (1998), iPod (2001), and iPad (2010). In 2007 he found a way to integrate all capabilities into a single terminal of an operating system, the iPhone.

- **Anneke Seley.** She is a sales guru who does not keep her knowledge all to herself. Apart from starting the innovate Sales 2.0 technique, she came up with Oracle Direct, a firm that helps sales teams accomplish their goals. (Discover more about the fifty best salespeople of all time at www.thankyouforselling.com.)

For You

Write down one thing that will improve your overall business or how you manage your team. What would it mean to you if you found a way to achieve this? Would it be satisfaction, financial, recognition, contribution, or promotion? This is the emotional reason why you will continue to pursue it until you achieve it.

Next, set up a timeline for what it is you wish to achieve.

It could be a day, week, month, or year. Finally, schedule it. This is the critical component. If you don't write it down, then there is a good chance it may not get completed. Your brain can be trained to understand that things you put in writing are important.

For Your Team

Ask your team to share their thoughts on what the phrase "Find a Way!" means to them.

Then, have a discussion on what the team or team members may be searching for in order to improve their business. Have each team member write down what they could do to focus on improving their business. Then have them spend time creating a strategy to finding a way to accomplish their outcome. I would recommend setting a timeline and action steps needed to accomplish their outcome. Review their progress in a future sales meeting.

Sometime after the "Find a Way" meeting, have a "Found a Way" meeting. It may be the following week or month, in six months, or later. Before the meeting, review the one thing you found a way to accomplish. During the meeting, ask your team members to do the same.

Have them walk through what they encountered and how they discovered a way to accomplish the outcome by answering the following questions:

- Why was it critical for them to find a way? This is the emotional reason why it was a must to find.
- Have them share the roadblocks and shortfalls they encountered.

- What did they discover about themselves?

- Did they have more focus, fun, or frustration?

- Ask the team any suggestions they would have if they were seeking the same thing.

After the team has had an opportunity to share their experiences, celebrate their accomplishments and progress!

Find a way to accomplish the one thing that could transform your business. You will learn so much about yourself through the process.

Chapter 36

GROW YOUR BUSINESS

I attended a Tony Robbins Business Mastery seminar that focused on strategies to lead your business effectively, efficiently, and profitably. He discussed Jay Abraham's three ways to grow a business:

1. Increase the number of customers (clients).
2. Increase the average transaction value.
3. Increase the frequency of repurchase—get more residual value out of each customer.

Which of Abraham's three ways to grow a business most appropriately matches your current business needs?

When reviewing your client list you may discover a variation of the strategies that will lead to more clients. In business, it's a common rule of thumb that 80 percent of your business will come from 20 percent of your clients. You will need to understand your numbers to know the best strategy to grow your revenue and, in return, your client's revenue.

You begin by knowing the number of customers, the average amount they spend, their repurchases, and the outcome you desire. Using the formula below, let's look at several examples:

Current # of customers x current average $ spent x current repurchase = total

Example one: 1,000 x $100 x 2= $200,000

Example two: Your outcome is to grow sales by 10%. 1,100 x $110 x 2.2 = $266,200 (33.1% revenue lift)

Example three: Your outcome is a 20% increase. 1,200 x 120 x 2.4 = $345,600 (72.8% revenue lift)

The results are exponential!

Keep in mind if your product is a one-time sale, you may instead count the number of referrals you get and convert to sale or consider adding an ongoing service to sell that can increase your frequency.

Taking the time upfront to identify where your opportunities are with your clients will pay big dividends for you. Discover which of the three options is the best strategy for you. Is it creating a new customer, getting that current client to spend more with you, or raising their average purchase with you?

Sara was brilliant at growing her income each year. She understood the principle that 80 percent of her income was generally generated from 20 percent of her accounts. Using this strategy, she would find ways to add other products and services to their current contract. She would find a way to lift her current clients by 10 percent over the prior year. She would discover areas of their business that needed additional focus and bring them solutions. She also knew the value of gaining a new customer. She created her top ten targets and developed a plan to convert them to new clients.

For You

Identify the clients who generate 80 percent of the company's revenue? Review each seller's client list and determine which accounts represent 80 percent of the seller's revenue. Using the process above, pinpoint which strategy would make the most impact for you. You may discover that 80 percent of your revenue is coming from 20 percent of your team.

For Your Team

Ask your team to share their thoughts on what the phrase "Grow Your Business" means to them. Have your team identify which of their clients generate 80 percent of their revenue. Using the strategy above, have them review and recommend which strategy would make the most impact on growing their client's business and, in return, would grow their own business.

"The grass is greener where you water it."

—*Neil Barringham*

Chapter 37

DO THE
FUNDAMENTALS

— — —

We all know the phrases "do the fundamentals" and "do the basics." The question is, how many of us do the fundamentals consistently? Doing only the very basics can be the difference to losing or earning business. When you master the basics you will become more effective in understanding your clients' needs; therefore you will be able to recommend better solutions for their outcomes. Follow these eight recommendations for each client to ensure you are doing the fundamentals.

1. **Winning attitude.** It starts with you visualizing your success. You see yourself accomplishing your outcomes day in and day out. You have extreme confidence in yourself and your abilities.

2. **Prospecting.** It's critical to your financial and personal growth. We need to shift our views on prospecting. We identify who the decision makers are on the accounts we are targeting. We focus our efforts in getting in front of them, not the non–decision makers.

3. **Probe.** Ask great questions to understand where your opportunity is to help the client. Being prepared with thoughtful questions based off the research you did prior to the call will set you apart from the rest.

4. **Presentation.** Make certain you present thoughtful solutions to your clients' needs. Your outcome is to overdeliver on their expectations. Spend time reviewing your notes from meetings to make certain your solutions solve their problems.

5. **Objections.** You will encounter various objections from your prospect. Anticipate those objections so you can answer any concerns the client may discuss. I would be prepared with a list of questions to ask your client, in the event you need additional information to better serve them. Sales is a process.

6. **Ask for the business.** You have done the work; now it's time to ask for the business. Most of us are great at building rapport and answering all the objections. You have earned the right to do business with them. Tenacity is the key.

7. **Make your mark.** Once the sale is complete, always follow up. You invested a lot of time and energy into gaining them as a customer. I would set up a system that matches the needs of your client. Some clients are very busy and may want weekly, monthly, or quarterly updates. Create a system that works so it is easy to stay connected.

8. **Recommendations.** A referred customer is already presold on you and your product. 91 percent of customers say they would give referrals, but only 11 percent of salespeople actually ask for them. We just need to ask![11]

One of my first managers in the business taught me a valuable lesson early on in my career. He would say, "Don't skip steps." At the time I was not really sure what he meant by the phrase. He had a forty-plus successful career in sales and shared with me that most sellers skip steps. He went on to explain that sellers meet clients and try to close them on the next call and then move to the next prospect. He said I may close a few clients with that system, but if I followed the fundamental steps of sales without skipping steps, I would create a lifetime of customers. He joined me on calls, and we followed these eight steps in the order listed. Today, I follow his system as a manager when on calls with my team. You develop partnerships, and clients see you as a resource.

For You

- Which of the fundamentals above are you your strongest?
- In which area could you use some coaching and growth?
- Identify some action steps you can take toward your improvement.

---

11 Dale Carnegie, "How Important are Sales Referrals for B2B Sales?," *Frontspin*, October 21, 2014.

For Your Team

Ask your team to share their thoughts on what the phrase "Do the fundamentals" means to them.

Next, identify each team member's strength from the fundamentals above. In which area could they use some coaching and growth? Identify action steps they can take toward their improvement.

*Going back to the basics strengthens
your foundation.*

Chapter 38

RAPPORT IS POWER

— — —

Rapport is created by having a feeling of commonality. We tend to create rapport more easily with people we are more alike than with those different from us. Think of your family, friends, coworkers, or clients whom you find it easy to communicate with. How is your rapport with those you have little in common with? A tremendous advantage you will have over the competition is the rapport you build with the customer. It's all about rapport and creating a trusting relationship with a prospect or a client currently doing business with you.

In order to build rapport quickly you need to learn to adapt to the person on the phone or to the person sitting across from you. The critical component is to be aware of how to communicate to that person. Here are five suggestions on how to improve your relationship:

1. **Build rapport:** Ask questions that are not related to sales. How is your day going? What would make it better?

Research the client on LinkedIn, Facebook, and Twitter, or Google the person to learn something you can create a conversation about. Find out which college they attended, if they like golf, their favorite music, if they have a family. You may ask how they got into their field of business.

2. **Auditory:** An auditory person absorbs verbal information by listening. When communicating with them you may notice them turning their ear toward you to hear what you're saying. You will be more successful communicating with an auditory person by being aware of your tone and the speed in which you communicate. The auditory person responds better when you use words like "sound," "hear," or "tell."

3. **Analytic:** An analytic person views the world through numbers and facts. They like to get to the bottom line on how things work and what the return on investment will be. An analytic person tends to be more reserved and quiet. You may want to talk slower and allow them the necessary time to review all data and benefits that your product offers. Therefore, earning their trust is key in earning their business.

4. **Visual:** A visual person loves to see things visually. They want you to show them through pictures or graphs. A visual person tends to communicate using their hands and facial expressions. Pay attention to the words they use, like: "show me," "see," "view," "focus," and "look." To be more successful when calling on visual clients, use phrases such as "I see," "This will show you," and "From my view."

5. **Kinesthetic:** A kinesthetic person tends to relate to how things feel. They communicate with emotion and

through expressions. You may notice that they look down to the right when communicating. A kinesthetic person tends to communicate by using words like: "touch," "feel," "grab," "connected," "sense," and "impression." When communicating with a kinesthetic, use words having to do with emotions.

When meeting with prospects or current clients, pay close attention to the words they use and their body language. You have an opportunity to instantly build rapport by adjusting the way you communicate with them. Becoming aware and mirroring the other person with the following suggestions can help create additional rapport:

- Tone of their voice
- Tempo of their voice
- Volume of their voice
- Posture and body language
- Gestures
- Facial expressions
- Eye contact
- Breathing pace
- The proximity of space between you

I called on an analytical client who was not interested in talking about the weather or the weekend. It was all about the numbers and results my product would deliver for the investment. My personality is more visual and expressive. I talk faster and have a lot of energy when communicating. My approach is more ideas and big-picture thinking, so I knew I had to adjust my approach when meeting this client. I found a way to connect with him instantly by starting our conversation on gross profit margins and how important it is to understand the company numbers. I spoke slowly, and my tone was confident. I asked him a question about how he evaluated his sales and his views on improving the overall efficiencies of the company. I was prepared with market trends and research that I knew would engage him. I was respectful of his time and asked If I could follow up with a second meeting after allowing him time to review all the data. I secured the second appointment and later provided solutions to outcomes.

For You

- How do you communicate with your team?
- Do you adjust your language pattern when trying to build rapport?
- When on sales calls, do you notice the words and expressions your client is communicating to you?
- How do you build rapport with clients who are different from you?

For Your Team

Ask your team to share their thoughts on what the phrase "Rapport Is Power" means to them.

Ask your team these questions:

- How do you build rapport with clients you're meeting for the first time?

- Are you paying attention to the words they are using and watching their body language?

- If you recently lost a sale, was it because you didn't earn their trust or build rapport?

- On your next call, notice the words the client is using when communicating with you. Are you adjusting to them to build better rapport?

> *"The most important thing in communication*
> *is to hear what isn't being said."*
> —*Peter Drucker*

Chapter 39

HOW'S YOUR FOCUS?

— — —

If you were to drive across the country on vacation, would you use a GPS or would you just put the car in drive and blindly hit the roads? You would use a GPS system, because it would provide you with a step-by-step guide to get you from point A to point B. By focusing on your ultimate goal and creating a step-by-step guide on how to get there, you will stay on the road to your ultimate destination (sales success!), and you will be less likely to end up lost in a part of town you don't want to be in (looking for another job).

Where do you focus your thoughts and actions? We've all heard the saying "You get what you focus on." Do you have a clear focus and road you need to take to exceed your goals? Or is your focus on fear and excuses for not being able to do what needs to be done? Your ability to focus sets the stage for where you will put your energy. Focus is a philosophy, not a resource.

I had a seller who had five hundred names on his list of accounts—some active clients, and the rest targets he hoped to secure. I asked the seller how he found the time to focus on that many accounts. He replied that he was always looking to grow his business each year. I coached the seller to consider breaking down the list of five hundred accounts into three areas:

1. Key accounts—currently spending over $250,000

2. Secondary accounts—currently spending $0-$249,999

3. Targets—not currently spending but could have potential

We discovered that he had lost focus on secondary accounts that had the potential to become key accounts. His time was spent on targets with very little opportunity, and it was taking his focus away from what he needed to accomplish to hit his revenue goals. We developed a plan that would allow him to service his key and secondary accounts and paired down the targets to his top twenty-five opportunities. We developed a strategy and timeline for each target. He became more focused and found he had more mental energy each day. He felt more in control of his business than ever before.

For You

- Decide what you need to focus on right now. What is a must for you to accomplish immediately?

- What actions do you need to focus on to achieve this outcome?

- Timeline your focus. Commit to keeping it as your focus until a certain time. If your goal is a small one, make the commitment period shorter. If your goal is long-term, make sure you have daily, weekly, or monthly outcomes until you achieve your goals.

- Execute your plan. This is a critical step to your success. We tend to lose focus or shift to something else when we meet a roadblock or setback. Stay the course and keep moving forward.

- Celebrate your success. Take the time to celebrate that you stayed focused on the goal you wanted to achieve.

For Your Team

Ask your team to share their thoughts on what the phrase "How's Your Focus?" means to them.

Next, ask your team the same questions you answered above. Then, ask them the following:

- Are you focused on what you want?

- How much time do you spend focusing on the outcome you are looking to achieve?

- Write down an example of something you wanted to achieve and accomplish.

"The key to success is to focus our conscious mind on the things we desire, not things we fear."
—*Brian Tracy*

Chapter 40

KEEP MOVING FORWARD!

—— —— ——

History is filled with people who achieved success after numerous attempts, such as Abraham Lincoln and Colonel Sanders (Kentucky Fried Chicken). The best salespeople know that a "no" is not permanent. Rather, they just have to keep moving forward in order to earn their business. And if they keep moving forward, they will discover what was keeping them from doing business with a particular client.

Most of us learned to ride a bicycle as a child. Numerous times we fell off our bike, only to get back up and try again. Most of us were determined; nothing would stop us from learning how to ride. Don't let a no hold you back from your sales success.

Here are several strategies that will help you keep moving forward during the sales process:

- Create a mindset of confidence and optimism.
- Get organized.

- Take control of your day.

- Prospect for clients whom you believe you can help.

- Put together a strategy for key or new clients.

- Handle the objections your client has that keep you from moving forward.

- Add another service product to your current client.

- Send a thank-you note to your current customers.

- Ask for a referral from a satisfied customer.

- Write a thank-you note to a fellow employee who goes the extra mile for you.

- Get out of your comfort zone.

- Believe you can!

- Invest in yourself. Listen to motivational messages to get your day started. Attend a seminar or read a book that inspires you.

There was a restaurant in town that had never advertised with our radio station, and we wanted to find out what was stopping us from working together. I sat down with the sales rep who handled that account and discussed what he had done to earn an appointment. Unfortunately, he'd done what most sellers do: He called without a valid business reason, took his "No!" from the owner, and then checked back in about four months. This process had been repeated for a couple of years. He didn't have forward momentum with the client; it was only start/stop.

Over the next three months, we worked out a systematic plan that included in-person visits in which we delivered articles relating to his industry, mailed hand-written notes, and shared success letters written by other restaurants. By using small steps that kept the sales process moving, we earned a sit-down meeting with the owner, discovered his needs, and put together a customized plan complete with a series of creative commercials that earned his business.

For You

- What do you need to do to keep moving your team forward?

- Is there an area of the sales process that is keeping your team from earning the client's business?

- Is there additional training you can provide to your team?

- Share an example with the team of a time you had to keep moving forward with a client and the steps you took.

For Your Team

Ask your team to share their thoughts on what the phrase "Keep Moving Forward!" means to them.

Next, walk your team through the following:

- Identify a client with whom you are stalled in the sales process.

- Do we understand what the business needs and where the opportunity is to help the business?

- What is one thing that could keep this sale moving forward?

- Are we meeting with the decision maker who has the authority to say yes to our solutions?

"Getting knocked down in life is a given. Getting up and moving forward is a choice.

—*Zig Ziglar*

Chapter 41

ARE YOU RELEVANT?

— — —

I recently read a blog that stated by 2020, 80 percent of B2B transactions will be automated, which means the number of sales jobs in the United States alone will shrink from its current 15.5 million to about 4.5 million.[12] I wondered if this would be the end to sales careers across the country. It made me realize how important it will be for the salesperson to remain relevant to the client if they plan to do business with them or, better yet, to remain in the field of sales. If this trend is true, it could mean there will be less focus on the product you're selling and more focus on you understanding your client's needs. One of my salespeople shared the news with me that she had lost a client's business to a competitor for the next year. We discussed the entire sales process to see if we could identify what we could have done differently to earn the client's business. The client shared that it was a very tough decision and he just felt

---

12 Laura Fagan, "4 Sales & Technology Trends Nobody is Talking About," Salesforce.com (blog), July 30, 2013. http://ww.salesforce.com/blog

he needed to go with the other company. We knew we had a year until our next opportunity to present for the business. To stay relevant, we designed a strategy of making sure we connected with the customer over the next twelve months. We sent bi-monthly industry-related articles that we felt would be helpful. We called each quarter, touching base to see how he was doing and how business was progressing. We created a Google alert account with his company name so we would be made aware of any major announcements. If the company received positive recognition, we sent a hand-written note of congratulations. We met the client for lunch occasionally to further establish rapport and let him know we were a trusted partner, even though we were not currently doing business. We wanted to make sure we were there as a resource and perhaps could be more visible than the company he selected over us.

Because we stayed close to the client, we were kept up to date with his business challenges and opportunities of solutions we could provide. We discovered a year later how we could win his business, and we did. We stayed top of mind with the client, and he appreciated the partnership we developed. He would often comment that he never had anyone provide him with ideas and strategies without needing to give them money. We knew it was a process, and we were willing to put the time and energy into this client. We won his business the next year and continued to stay relevant years after.

For You

- How do you stay relevant with your key accounts?
- What strategies are you implementing to be relevant to prospects you are targeting?

- Have each sales person create their game plan for staying relevant to their key accounts, secondary accounts, and target accounts.

- How can you use technology to your advantage in staying relevant and winning business?

For Your Team

Ask your team to share their thoughts on what the phrase "Are You Relevant?" means to them.

Next, lead your team through the following:

- Ask if they feel they are relevant to their clients.

- Ask them to list the best ways to stay connected to key clients.

- Break down the list into three categories: key accounts, secondary accounts, and prospects. Create a strategy for each category of the best way to stay relevant to those clients. Determine how often you will connect with them and what you will do to stay relevant to them.

- Come up with a list of technology, such as Google alerts, your team can use to stay relevant.

> *"Remember that the six most expensive words in business are: We've always done it that way."*
> —*Catherine DeVrye*

Chapter 42

NEVER UNDERESTIMATE YOURSELF!

— — —

Have you ever been warned not to sell yourself short? We all know that doing so would mean that you were underestimating your abilities and that your confidence wouldn't be where it should be. Perhaps you developed this habit through time and you were not even aware of it. This may have happened early in your life. For example, not raising your hand in school if you knew the answers, or being afraid to share your ideas at work in sales meetings for fear others would not like your concepts. So you sit back and let others speak up and share their ideas. Each time you give in to underestimating yourself, you are reinforcing the notion that you and your ideas are not good enough, that you're not capable enough.

So how can you stop underestimating yourself? Think of times you did succeed. We all have something we have succeeded in doing. Can you remember your first sale? Is there something you personally succeeded in doing? You can use these experiences to reinforce that you are capable of achieving great things.

Stop comparing yourself to other people. We each have our own talents and abilities to offer. When you underestimate yourself, you limit your life experiences. You hold yourself back from accomplishing your goal, and you find reasons not to move forward. As a leader, creating an environment that encouraged everyone to share their thoughts will give you access to some potentially fresh and powerful ideas.

A manager's position became available and I decided to apply for it. I had been in sales, but I had no management experience. I was competing against many others who had management experience. It would have been easy for me to dismiss my abilities to lead the team and self-talk myself right out of the position. I went a different direction and began to focus on what I had accomplished the past ten years in sales. I reinforced my past experiences of success and thought about how I could use those experiences in a managerial role. I had to believe in myself and my abilities to lead others.

I began to think about all the managers I had been exposed to and their redeeming qualities that impacted me throughout my career. I had the ability to tap into those great leaders and add my own thoughts and strategy of how I could help others and earn the position. I told myself that if I were given the opportunity to lead, I would make a difference. I was given that opportunity, and I never took it for granted. Each day I gained more confidence from each experience. I knew I had to believe in my abilities and give myself a chance to step into this big role. I am glad I never underestimated myself!

For You

- How do you encourage others to share their ideas? Asking questions beginning with "Why?" or "What do you think?" will set the stage for your team to discover possible solutions, build confidence, and encourage them to think and share.

- Is there a platform you can create to tap into ideas from others on your team?

- Do you have a platform to share your ideas with your boss?

For Your Team

Ask your team to share their thoughts on what the phrase "Never Underestimate Yourself!" means to them.

Next, ask your team the following:

- Write down one example of where you may have doubted your abilities and pushed through to a successful outcome.

- Share why you succeeded.

- What is one idea that we are not currently doing that you believe can help our company?

- Are there better systems we can create to be more productive each day?

Never underestimate what you can accomplish
when you believe in yourself.

Chapter 43

YOUR BIG BREAKTHROUGH

— — —

Is there something that is creating a barrier from you achieving your outcomes? It may be something you're not even aware of. You may encounter challenges to meeting your revenue expectations at some point in your sales career. However, if you can become aware of what may be holding you back, you have the opportunity to overcome those challenges and resist letting those barriers stop you from achieving sales. What you will discover is that once you break through that barrier, you gain confidence and energy for other situations you may face.

There are three things you need clarity on:

1. **Focus.** This is you identifying the one thing you need to change or break through. The one thing keeping you and your business from growing. What needs to be accomplished right now? Do you see the glass half full or half empty? If you focus on what's not working, you're more likely to get more of what's not working. It's your mindset:

what you put your energy into and what you focus on. Write down what you would like to break through with your business and post it in a place where you will see it throughout your workday. Possible answers could be setting more new business meetings; calling on clients with larger budgets; selling more product or service lines; and creating more commissions.

2. **Self-talk.** What's the dialogue you're having with yourself? You may need to shift your thinking patterns and this dialogue. Do you feel optimistic or pessimistic? Are you focused on fear of rejection or are you confident? What happens is that your self-dialogue directs your focus. Most of us are not aware of our self-talk. I recommend you choose your words wisely and perhaps consider replacing them with the following: "I got this! I am excited to help companies grow their businesses! I am confident! I have the experience, and I have helped other companies succeed. I work smart. I am effective. Yes, I can! Yes, I will!"

3. **Physical expression.** Our body guides our emotions. It's biochemistry. If you want to be confident, start standing tall, with your head up, and walk with purpose. Have positive energy and smile. Do you walk with purpose or are you wandering around to avoid what needs to get addressed so your business can move forward? What you tell your mind to express to others is revealed through your body language.

One big breakthrough I witnessed occurred when I met with one of my salespeople who wanted to prospect accounts with bigger budgets. He tended to focus his time and effort on prospecting smaller companies that most often didn't have the resources on a consistent basis to market their company. He felt more comfortable and confident meeting companies of that size. He was great at building rapport, and the clients loved him. He would find himself meeting with them multiple times, sharing big ideas only to be disappointed that they didn't have the resources to invest with him. This situation would have him falling short on his budgets each month because so much time was spent with them.

In our weekly meeting, we discussed what he thought may be holding him back from calling on larger accounts. He thought for a minute and then replied that he didn't like cold-calling on big accounts for fear of rejection. I wasn't surprised by his response. I pointed out that he had over twenty years of media experience and the big clients could benefit from his creativity. I asked what it would mean to him financially when he closed a major account. He said he could pay down debt, fund his kid's college education, and finally take his wife on a well-deserved vacation. Over the next few weeks we spent time creating a list of major accounts that he would call on. We spent time focusing on valid business reasons for the companies to work with us. We role-played the phone calls so he could gain confidence and tell himself that his experience could be a game changer for the company he targeted. Then he put it into action. He would stand up with a big smile on his face when making his calls. His energy was contagious, and he was successful setting appointments with big accounts. He had a major breakthrough! And he did surprise his wife with an incredible vacation.

For You and Your Team

A great team-building exercise to do with your team is helping them have a big breakthrough. You will need to purchase a few items. Order the thin, soft white-pine boards that you can easily break. They should be 9" by 1" planks. You will also need markers to write on the boards. There are examples on the Internet of how to hold the boards so they break easily. Give everyone a board and a marker. The wood will serve as a metaphor for the obstacles or barriers in the way of achieving their outcomes. On the front of the board, ask your team to write their big breakthrough, the one thing holding them back from achieving their goals.

On the other side of the board, have your team write what it would mean to them if they broke that barrier. What would the outcome be? Examples: fear of setting new calls. What it would mean to you and your family when you master appointment setting. How much money you would make every month, every year? Do you see yourself in your new house, driving your new car, taking an exotic vacation, paying for your kid's college education, weddings for your children, your retirement?

Cheer for each team member as they break through what has been keeping them from moving forward. I recommend that the manager hold each board and high-five the team members once they break through it.

"Sales are contingent upon the attitude of the salesperson—not the attitude of the prospect."

—*W. Clement Stone*

Chapter 44

CONSISTENCY PAYS OFF

— — —

Successful businesses are defined by consistency, by doing the same thing, the same way, with the same result every time. Think about McDonald's. No matter where in the world you visit a McDonald's, you can expect the same product prepared the same way and delivering the same flavor.

Consistency is critical to any sales team. Your clients expect and deserve to be treated the same way every time (assuming, of course, that they are being treated with excellence!). But let's dig a little deeper. Here are some thoughts on why consistency is critical to business success:

- Consistent sellers work against very high standards. They have an approach to business and to client service that sets them apart from other sellers.

- Consistent sellers embrace accountability. They thrive on the knowledge that their clients view them with high expectations.

- Consistent sellers know they are relevant. They realize that their success, over time, is what separates them from others.

- Consistent sellers have an excellent reputation. They want to be respected by their clients.

- Consistent sellers love to be measured. They embrace challenges and being pushed to grow.

- Consistent sellers have a message. They are known for how clearly and effectively they communicate.

- Consistent sellers are superior listeners. They understand that customers want to be heard and understood.

Consistency is driven by confidence. The best sellers are self-aware of their talents and work hard to build upon these talents over time. They understand that patterns of behavior are important. But, perhaps most importantly, they embrace two realities of successful business:

- Success is driven by repeatedly satisfying customers with ideas and service.

- Success is closely tied to reliability; customers know they can depend on you for the same performance every time.

I hired a new salesperson for my team. She was different from most sellers I had hired. She had transferred from another city to be a nanny for the summer. After the summer, she planned to look for full-time employment. I agreed to an interview after she had been so persistent at meeting with me for the sales position. She was smart, knowledgeable about our radio stations, and asked great questions during the interview. I understood that I might be taking a risk in hiring someone with little sales experience, but there was something about how consistent she was with her follow-up with me that I was willing to give her an opportunity. I was glad I did, as she built a very successful career at the radio stations.

The key to her success was that she was consistent with how she approached each day. She came to work at the same time (before all other sellers). If I walked by her desk and she wasn't sitting there by 7:30 a.m., I thought something had happened to her. She made new business calls every day in addition to servicing her current clients. She was consistent with her clients, and they appreciated it. She would think of one creative idea each week that she could take to prospective clients or current clients to lift their spending with her. Her consistent approach paid off big dividends to her and our company.

For You

- Are you consistent on a daily basis when managing your team?
- Is your team consistent on meeting or exceeding their expectations?
- Can you identify an area of your business where you could be more consistent?
- How consistent is your product or service with your clients?

For Your Team

Ask your team to share their thoughts on what the phrase "Consistency Pays Off" means to them.

Next, discuss "Consistency Pays Off" with your team by using these prompts:

- Think of someone you know (other than yourself, of course) who is extremely successful. In what ways does consistency play a role in their success?

- What do you do most consistently, and how does it pay off?

- How can you improve your consistency when it comes to delivering superior results for your clients?

- What can you do more consistently to improve your personal life?

If you are persistent, you will get it. If you are consistent, you will keep it.

Chapter 45

ACTIVITY WITH PRODUCTIVITY

— — —

We may fill our days with many activities. The question is, do the activities have productivity? Is there a measureable outcome at the end of each day? When we focus on what we need to accomplish in order to achieve our goals, are we using our time wisely?

In a weekly one-on-one meeting with one of my account executives I asked how his appointment setting was going. He replied that he spent hours each day prospecting and calling clients to set up meetings, though he usually set up only a few. He said he wasn't more productive because he was often bounced into voicemail and wasn't able to connect to the decision maker on the phone. When he did connect with the decision maker, he stumbled with asking the right questions to secure the appointment.

I asked him to show me his prospect list and for each potential client to include one or two reasons why that client should put us on their calendar. We worked on a script to give him confidence so he would be prepared for the call with the decision maker. We scheduled blocks of time each day to make calls, and we reviewed all calls at the end of the day. We began to see how many calls he would need to schedule an appointment. We tracked his progress and discovered he would need to make twenty calls to connect with five decision makers, and from there he was successful in scheduling new appointments. He recorded each call with his cell phone so we could review his tone of voice and language. We gained a better understanding of what was working for him when he set a new business appointment.

For You

- What activities do you find yourself focusing on each day or each week that impact your production?
- Do the activities distract you from your outcomes each week?
- What strategies can you implement to be more productive?

For Your Team

Ask your team to share their thoughts on what the phrase "Activity with Productivity" means to them. Next, have your team list all the activities they do during a workday, such as interacting with coworkers, sending emails, prospecting, returning phone calls, seeing customers, writing up customer orders, handling daily issues, etc. Ask them to review the list and place a *P* for "productivity" next to each activity that produces results. "Results" means the outcome they're looking for when doing the activity. For example, they would place a *P* next to "Prospecting," because prospecting is how they schedule their first appointment.

Ask your team what they noticed or discovered from reviewing their list of activities. How many *P*s were listed in a day? It's easy to fall into the trap of being active without being productive.

Now ask your team to list productive things they could do each day. What produces the results or outcomes for them each day? Next look at each productive activity and determine if the desired results were obtained. For example, if it took eight times to schedule the first meeting with a new business prospect, are there recommendations you can make and coach the salesperson to schedule the meeting sooner? Ask your team to brainstorm possible solutions and be prepared to offer some as well.

Being busy means doing stuff; being productive
means getting stuff done!

Chapter 46

IT'S YOUR CHOICE

The power to choose! Just that phrase is a powerful statement. Various Internet sources estimate that an adult makes about 35,000 remotely conscious decisions each day. This number may sound absurd, but in fact, we make 226.7 decisions each day about food alone, according to researchers at Cornell University.[13] What will you choose to do today?

I met with an account executive who appeared overwhelmed at the end of each day. I asked how I could help, and she complained that she didn't feel there was enough time in the day to accomplish all that she wanted to accomplish. I wrote down all the things she felt she needed to accomplish that day: following up on proposals, returning emails, internal meetings, outside calls, conference calls, and updating projections. We reviewed the tasks, and I asked

---

13 Brian Wansink and Jeffery Sobal, "Mindless Eating: The 200 Daily food decisions we overlook," *Environment and Behavior* 39:1 (2007): 106-123.

her to choose which would benefit her business the most. I reminded her that every day we have to make choices.

For You

- What decisions/choices do you need to make to improve your performance and the performance of your team?
- Can you identify areas of opportunities for your team?
- Have you prioritized the decisions that will have the biggest impact on your business?
- What have you learned from bad decisions you have made?
- What would you do differently next time?
- How can this experience help you make better choices next time?

For Your Team

Ask your team to share their thoughts on what the phrase "It's Your Choice" means to them.

Next, ask them to think about what choices they need to make right now. What are the options they are considering? Could it be any of the following:

- Do you need additional training?
- Do you need to prospect more meaningful customers?
- Do you need support?

- Do you need more focus?
- Do you need to be more organized?
- Do you need to stop making excuses?
- Do you need to spend more time developing your customer relationships?
- Do you need to step out of your comfort zone?
- Do you need to just take the step?

It really doesn't matter where each team member is as long as they know they have the power to choose. You can encourage them by asking what is stopping them from moving forward. The power to act lies within each of your team members. How rewarding it is to know that we all have options and the ability to create our own roadmap to success!

Make a decision, and give it your full attention
for the best outcome.

Chapter 47

OUTCOME = INCOME

— —— —

Most who enter the fields of sales or management are driven by money. In order to exceed your income expectations, it takes a certain number of outcomes. The statement "You get out what you put in" puts everything into perspective.

Janet, a saleswoman in the media industry, approached me about making more money. She was generating $85,000 a year but wanted to make a six-figure income, which meant she needed to create an additional $15,000. Together we discovered her average account was worth $4,250 income; therefore, she would need to develop three new accounts or grow her current accounts. She made the decision to grow her business with new accounts. We created a strategy and timeline to help guide her. She focused her efforts on prospecting and set a goal of three new meetings each week. She now understood it was a numbers game, and she would need to call a certain amount of clients who would have the ability to spend with her. She blocked time on her calendar and titled it "Three to thrive" to remind her of the three meetings she needed to accomplish each day to reach the income she desired. Her commitment to plan and her execution of the calls led her to exceeding her income.

For You

Prepare a list that you can hand out in the meeting detailing the amount each account generates from an income perspective. Be prepared to share a fictional example of the necessary game plan needed to achieve a desired income.

For Your Team

Ask your team to share their thoughts on what the phrase "Outcome = Income" means to them.

Next, lead the team in a discussion about the outcomes you want to achieve as a team and how each of them achieving their personal outcome contributes to the overall team outcome. For example, you could discuss any or all of the following:

- As an organization, do we need to prospect smarter? Are we using LinkedIn and client referrals from those customers who are happy working with us?

- Replacing the phrase "cold-calling" with "treasure hunting" or "power hour" can be a simple shift in the mind of a salesperson when scheduling calls.

- Focus on prospecting for a new client who has spending potential.

- Have you leveraged your support team to allow yourself more time to retain or grow current clients?

- Have you shared research or an industry article that could spark an idea to help your client?

- Have you written current clients, thanking them for their business?

- What will you do differently to make an impact on your outcomes?

- How will you achieve your outcomes?

- When will you achieve your outcomes? Create a timeline to hold yourself accountable.

Work hard for what you want because it won't come to you without a plan and action. You have to be confident and know you can do anything you set your mind to.

Chapter 48

JUST GET STARTED

— — —

Getting started at times is the hardest action item for us to do on a consistent basis. In sales, we encounter multiple levels of maybe or no that stop us from moving forward. It's human behavior for us to avoid rejection or the thought that someone is not interested in what we have to offer, so we tend to go where we are more comfortable and familiar. Our minds are powerful, and they can create exaggerated thoughts that cause us to pause or not get started.

Every outcome we accomplish began with starting. In most cases, starting began with small steps and accomplishments along the way that built confidence in us. At times when we focus on the big picture, it can overwhelm us and we become mentally exhausted—so we delay getting started. In some cases, we don't start at all. I recommend that you just start doing to create the momentum. You will discover that you will gain energy and confidence along the way. This major obstacle you created becomes a stepping-stone to your success.

I was meeting with a senior-level salesperson who experienced a year of major account attrition and was having challenges meeting his goals. I could see he was overwhelmed with the pressure to perform and hit his budgets. He was having issues getting started on discovering new accounts that could close the gap of his monthly shortfalls. The ability to make up the billing was so overwhelming he would find himself going back to the accounts currently spending and not focus on developing new accounts.

In our discussion, we realized that he needed to get started by targeting one new account each day. He had to set new meeting with prospects so he could replace the business that was not returning. He realized the importance of what needed to be done and made a decision to start each day setting a new business meeting with a new client. He understood it was a process and getting started was the only way!

For You

At times, getting started is all mental. You have to set your intention mentally first and then get started with action steps. Are there small steps you can start taking now to improve your sales? Can you identify where your team should start? What opportunities have you identified that, if you started them today, would impact your bottom line?

Below are suggestions on how to get your mind in gear and start taking action. **Just start.** By starting something and getting a flow going, you'll be able to get your brain in the game. You need to just pick one task or project and begin.

- **Make a list of what needs to be done.** The key is to capture it in writing so you commit to doing

something. You can create momentum from simply
starting.

- **Start with an achievable goal.** Whatever you need to
  get started on, I recommend breaking it down into
  small accomplishments each day until it's completed.
  We can commit to doing something each day by
  understanding it's a process. You will gain confidence
  as you achieve this goal.

For Your Team

Ask your team the following:

- Can you identify one thing that, if you just got
  started on it, would impact your sales?
- What are some things you spend too much time on
  that stall your business? Is it possible to eliminate
  those tasks so you can focus your efforts on other,
  more profitable areas of your business?

> *"Start where you are. Use what you have.*
> *Do what you can."*
> —*Arthur Ashe*

Chapter 49

ACTIVITY AND EFFECTIVENESS

— — —

I had the pleasure of meeting Steve Mulch, owner of the Veritas Training Group. He shared the benefits of companies understanding the power of how the words "activity and effectiveness" can improve their team's sales performance, a methodology that has transformed thousands of sales organizations.

These three words can define the sales outcome of your organization. Understanding where your team is performing gives you a great opportunity to coach them to a better outcome. The key is to have the right activity and effectiveness to produce maximum sales.

Many of us at some point of our careers will fall into one of the following categories:

- Activity + effectiveness = big sales

This means you have great activity with meeting with multiple clients and you're effective at closing them, which equals big sales.

- Big activity + little effectiveness = small sales

You have great activity with meeting clients, but fall short on being effective in moving the sale along. You become more of a professional visitor and are challenged at closing the client. Your calendar is full of busy tasks and few sales.

- Little activity + big effectiveness = small sales

You focus your efforts on a few clients with whom you created great relationships, so you're able to close them. You have a small pipeline of clients, however, so sales are small.

Which category best describes where you are today? Do you see a pattern of where your team is performing? The key is to understand your activities and how effective you are at moving your business forward and the necessary adjustments you need to make to improve your performance.

I love the game of golf. If you have played golf, you understand that to be effective you need to spend time practicing so you're prepared when you play. Putting is an area of your game that can help you produce a really good score. Improving your score will require you to practice short, uphill, downhill, or sidehill putts to be effective. There are so many components: whether you are lined up correctly; the speed of the ball; how you stand over the ball; and the roll of the putt. Taking the time to practice will help you gain strength and confidence to putt the ball. You practice a shot over and over in order to be prepared and effective.

In sales it is no different. There are normally a few objections that are common and then there are a few that come out of the blue. When you are stumped, you lose confidence; and when you lose confidence, it is hard to convince someone to do business with you. We all go through it. The best lesson I ever learned about answering client objections was from Ronnie. His confidence, poise, and ability to answer any question came from not just making mistakes but practicing for better results the next time.

Early in my career, I was that salesperson who would leave a call and miss an opportunity to sell because I was not effective in answering an objection. I made a decision to follow Ronnie's success model and understand the top objections I could face on a call. I practiced by anticipating them and saying them out loud on my way to calls. I practiced so much you could wake me up in the middle of the night and I would be able to answer them effortlessly. It takes practice to be the most effective.

For You and Your Team

Ask your team to share their thoughts on what the phrase "Activity and Effectiveness" means to them.

Make a note of it if you feel you need to add more activities to your day. How can you become more effective on calls? Have you lost business due to not being prepared for the call?

If your outcome is to have activity and effectiveness for big sales, your definition of a good day might be adding one new meaningful prospect and moving one of your clients forward in the sales process. I recommend asking your team for ideas on how they could improve their activity and effectiveness each day.

Ask your team to review their past week by writing on one page all the activities they completed. Next, have them circle the activities where they thought they were effective.

For example: I met with client A, so I circle it because I was able to secure the next call to present a proposal. In another example they might list client B, but the call does not have a next step because the call has stalled. In this case they would not circle it.

Next, you and your team should review your week to see where the opportunities are to improve your business. Is there something that needs practice to improve your effectiveness? In order to master sales, it takes the right activities to produce effective results. We can benefit from each interaction we have with clients by learning from each call.

Begin by always being prepared and expecting good things to happen to you.

Chapter 50

DO IT AGAIN!

Practice is doing something again and again in order to become better at it. Most of us have heard the phrase "practice makes perfect." Team USA gymnasts spend an average of thirty hours per week training. Three days a week they have two practices a day. In addition to their training they have to go to the gym and go to school. They practice their routines over and over for the one moment they perform. With each practice, they identify how they can improve and get better.

Can you imagine spending thirty hours a week practicing your field of business? It may not be realistic to spend thirty hours a week practicing the one thing you need to improve in your business, but I am certain you could find thirty minutes to an hour each day to focus on practicing in the area of your business that could use a little boost. Is there something you can identify that you need to practice to improve your bottom line? Here are the key attributes of those who tend to win year after year:

- **Leadership.** A leader is a person who others follow. They have heart, integrity, ability, confidence, and the will to win. Do you have a winning mindset?

- **Goal-oriented.** Those who win know when they achieve their goals. They are always looking for ways to improve themselves. Excellence is a way of life for them.

- **The roadmap.** You develop an effective plan that leads you down the road to reaching your goals. You're always learning along the way from your efforts.

- **The will.** Those who practice again and again always evaluate their performance to determine what they can do better next time and to discover what they gained from the experience.

I was once on a call when the client started our "meeting" by saying, "I'm not interested." Of course my first reaction was to ask why. Then I rambled on about how great my product was, how our product was the best in the industry, blah, blah, blah. I blew the meeting. As I reflected on the call, I realized that I had not been prepared. I had rambled on about my product, but not about the needs of the client. Do you remember a time when you got cornered with an objection, and instead of replying with a fluid, confident response you stumbled because the objection caught you off guard? By mastering the common objections, memorizing the rebuttal, and practicing over and over again, you will become comfortable with your response and gain credibility in your industry.

For You

Ask yourself what you need to do again to keep your business moving forward, your team growing, and your customers renewing. What areas of your business have you identified that need practice? Identify the areas in which each team member may need to sharpen their skills.

For Your Team

Ask your team to share their thoughts on what the phrase "Do It Again!" means to them.

Next, ask them to share examples of things they are great at during the sales process. Is it prospecting, asking great questions, handling objections, leading presentations, or closing the sale? Ask them to share examples of things they need improvement on during the sales process. What actions do they need to take to improve? How much time each day will you dedicate to perfecting your skill level?

"Just do it. Then do it again."

—*Nike*

Chapter 51

WHAT DRIVES YOU?

— — —

Have you stopped to think about what drives you to accomplish your goals—both personally and professionally? Whatever your outcome is you must understand the *why*. The why is the emotional reason we do what we do. The why is the fuel to our fire.

Depending on your outcomes, the factors that drive you will be different from those of others. However, we all tend to be enticed by one or more of the following:

- Recognition and respect from others
- Money
- Security (job, financial)
- Power or prestige
- Independence (feeling in charge of your own life)
- Opportunity to improve, grow, and become more

- Contribution (wanting to make a difference in the lives of others)
- Ambition
- Competitiveness (you have the need to win every time)

We can agree that others can inspire, encourage, support, or coach us. However, you are the only one who can drive you. Below is a list of character traits that those with drive possess:

- **Confidence.** The confident person learns how to build their confidence. They recognize their shortcomings and seek coaching to compensate. They keep pursuing their outcomes.
- **Persistence.** The persistent person will find a solution for most of the hurdles they encounter. They don't let obstacles get in their way, and they keep moving forward.
- **Determination.** The determined person has a plan, and nothing and no one can stand in their way.
- **Focus.** The driven person is focused on their outcome and is seldom distracted from it.
- **Energy.** The energetic person has a lot of enthusiasm. They tend to walk fast, with a purpose, and are full of life.
- **Knowledge.** The knowledgeable person does their research and knows the game. They are seen as the expert in their field, and they always strive to learn more.

- **Faith.** The faithful person sees the world brimming with possibilities and envisions positive outcomes. They believe in something bigger than themselves.

I hired a woman with very little experience to join our sales team. Most of the salespeople and other managers thought I was crazy to do so, because of her lack of sales experience. But she had something that is difficult to find in others—energy and enthusiasm. (She had a Southern drawl as well, which made her even more endearing.) I assumed I could teach her the sales side of the business.

She learned the business very quickly and even took online classes to become certified in marketing to perfect her skill set. She was extremely focused on her plan each day and approached the day as if it were her last. She realized failure was not an option for her. Her enthusiasm spread across the sales floor as her coworkers witnessed her work ethic and tenacity. She took full advantage of the opportunity she was given and was extremely successful.

For You

- What are the factors that drive you?
- Which character traits above best describe you?
- How can you expand on this knowledge to benefit yourself and your team?

For Your Team

Ask your team to share their thoughts on what the phrase "What Drives You?" means to them.

Next, ask them which character traits best describe them. Discuss how they can harness that knowledge to benefit themselves as well as their business.

"It's not what you do; it's why you do it!"
—*Simon Sinek*

Chapter 52

NOW, NEXT, THEN

— — —

Most of us are overwhelmed with too much to do in too little time. We struggle to get caught up as new tasks and responsibilities are added each day. Because of this we always seem to fall behind and never feel accomplished. In order to take control of the situation, we need to create a system that will help us manage through the process. This process is called "Now, Next, Then." These three words keep you focused on the right activities to improve or grow your business. It helps guide you to determine what actions are necessary for you to achieve your outcomes. You will feel empowered as you track your progress. Below, we will review the meaning of these words and how to implement them.

1. **Now.** Develop a routine for identifying what outcome needs attention right now. What have you decided is a priority to be accomplished now?

2. **Next.** What strategies and timelines have you set in order to accomplish this outcome? What should be worked on first that can't wait and could improve your business?

3. **Then.** It's time to take action on your plan. Once you complete that need, move forward to your next outcome.

Once you take the step toward the one thing on your list holding you back, you should have more confidence and energy. We can mentally drain ourselves by putting off something we know needs to get done. You will gain momentum each time you accomplish the task you have been putting off.

At some point in your management career you will have to work with employees to coach them to a better performance, to a level of success, in order for them to maintain their position. Now, Next, Then is a great opportunity to help coach an employee falling short on his goals and guide him through the process.

I worked with a ten-year veteran salesperson who was missing his monthly budgets, which lead to missing his quarterly goals. He faced a large amount of key account attrition for the quarter, which was impacting his year. The task of hitting his budgets seemed daunting. I knew I had to find a way to break down this major endeavor, piece by piece, so he could finish the year respectfully. We met to discuss the key accounts not returning and what he would need to do to begin to chip away at the deficit each day.

We began by identifying his top twenty targets that we felt confident we could help. We agreed that he would block time out each day on his calendar to set the new appointments. Next we agreed to a timeline of getting in front of the twenty targets. We met with each target and created a marketing plan to gain their business. Then we created a sense of urgency to earn their business. We were able to secure twelve out of twenty accounts to work with us, and the other eight looked promising to work with us the following year. My seller gained more confidence and discovered how much fun it was to connect with clients and build a solid relationship. He succeeded by refining each situation and gained confidence along the way.

For You

- Think of what needs attention now with your business.

- Are you satisfied with your performance and your team's performance?

- How engaged are you right now in accomplishing your outcomes?

- What is your vision now for you and your team?

- Assess each team member to see where they are now, what their next step is, and what you want to see them accomplish. You'll soon see results—based on the coaching and direction you gave them.

For Your Team

- Ask your team to share their thoughts on what the phrase "Now, Next, Then" means to them.

Next, ask them the following questions:

- What does "now" mean to you?
- What would you need to do next?
- How soon will you implement this action plan? When will you achieve this, and what is your timeline for accomplishing this?
- What result will you realize from doing this?
- Is there a client/customer who needs your attention now?

If not now, when? Now is the time to stop putting off what can move you and your business forward.

ACKNOWLEDGMENTS

— — —

This is a very personal book, so let me end it on a personal note.
Life is about making connections. I am grateful to the connections I have created. I have learned so much from those experiences and have grown immensely from the thousands of sales professionals and managers I've worked with throughout my career. You have helped inspire me to live my best version of myself.

To my readers, what an honor and privilege to write a book for you—a book that I hope saves you time each week and engages, inspires, and empowers you.

In particular, I would like to thank my wife, Olivia, for her encouragement and support. Thank you to those who helped me realize my dream of sharing a simple concept of Three-Word Meetings so other leaders could use or share the content with their teams: my twin sister, Lynn; sister Tracy; my mom; and my dear friends Sharon, Monica, and Leah. My coworkers, who inspire me to be a better leader every day: Christine Mello, Doug Smith, and Doug Spak; and the sales and programming leaders at WKRQ, WREW, and WUBE/WYGY.

I hope you create your own three words in addition to the ones I have created so that you stay inspired, engaged, and continue empowering others!

ABOUT THE AUTHOR

 **Lisa Thal** has been in media sales and management since 1987. She is currently a General Sales Manager at WKRQ in Cincinnati, owned by Hubbard Media, where she has the privilege of coaching talented sales professionals.

In addition to working in management, she is also a certified life coach. Her 2015 book, *Why I Chose You*, is an inspirational guide that helps readers find clarity by understanding why they've chosen certain people and relationships in their lives.

Lisa loves golf and enjoying the outdoors, and she cherishes her health, family, friendships, wife, Olivia, and her three fur kids—Phoenix, Dakota, and Denali. This is her second book.